RUST PROGRAMMING MASTERY:

FROM BEGINNER TO EXPERT IN SYSTEMS PROGRAMMING

FIRST EDITION

Preface

Rust has gained significant traction in the systems programming world due to its focus on memory safety, performance, and concurrency. This book aims to guide both beginners and experienced developers through the language's unique features and its applications in real-world scenarios.

Throughout this book, readers will explore the fundamental principles of Rust, including ownership, borrowing, and lifetimes, which set it apart from other programming languages. We will delve into Rust's memory management model, which eliminates common bugs such as null pointer dereferencing and data races. Additionally, we will cover collections, iterators, and advanced type features that allow for flexible and efficient code.

A major focus of this book is Rust's approach to concurrency, enabling developers to write safe and scalable multithreaded applications. We will examine key concurrency primitives, such as Mutex, Arc, and RwLock, as well as Rust's powerful async/await model for handling asynchronous operations.

Beyond the core language features, this book explores Rust's applications in systems programming, including low-level memory manipulation, writing efficient embedded code, and interfacing with C. We will also dive into Rust's growing ecosystem for web and network programming, covering frameworks like Actix and Rocket, as well as networking libraries such as Tokio.

Performance optimization and debugging techniques are crucial for writing high-performance Rust applications. This book will introduce profiling tools, common performance pitfalls, and methods for identifying and resolving bottlenecks.

Finally, we will discuss best practices for writing maintainable and scalable Rust code in production environments. Security, CI/CD pipelines, and real-world case studies will provide insights into how Rust is being adopted in industries ranging from embedded systems to large-scale cloud applications.

By the end of this book, readers will have a deep understanding of Rust's capabilities and how to leverage them to build safe, high-performance, and concurrent applications. Whether you are a systems programmer, web developer, or performance enthusiast, Rust offers a powerful toolset for modern software development.

Table of Contents

Chapter 1: Introduction to Rust and Systems Programming

Understanding Systems Programming

Systems programming involves writing software that provides services to other software or directly interfaces with hardware. Unlike application programming, where developers focus on user-facing software, systems programming emphasizes performance, efficiency, and direct resource management.

Why Systems Programming Matters

Systems programming is the foundation of operating systems, databases, network services, and embedded systems. Writing efficient and reliable system software requires control over memory, CPU resources, and low-level hardware interactions.

Key characteristics of systems programming:

- **Performance**: Systems software often runs close to the hardware and must be highly optimized.
- **Low-Level Access**: Systems programming languages provide fine-grained control over memory and CPU registers.
- **Concurrency and Parallelism**: Many systems software components need to handle multiple tasks simultaneously.
- **Memory Safety**: Avoiding common memory errors such as buffer overflows, use-after-free, and race conditions is critical.

Traditionally, C and C++ have been the dominant languages for systems programming, but they come with inherent risks such as manual memory management, undefined behavior, and data races in multithreaded programs.

The Rise of Rust in Systems Programming

Rust offers an alternative that balances performance and safety without sacrificing expressiveness. Rust's key innovations include:

- **Ownership System**: Prevents memory leaks and data races at compile time.
- **Borrow Checker**: Ensures references do not outlive the data they point to.
- **Zero-Cost Abstractions**: Allows developers to write high-level code without performance penalties.
- **Concurrency Safety**: Enables fearless concurrency with built-in synchronization primitives.

Rust is increasingly being adopted in domains where reliability and performance are crucial, including:

- **Operating Systems**: Rust is used in projects like Redox OS and parts of the Linux kernel.
- **Embedded Systems**: The Rust ecosystem includes frameworks like `embedded-hal` for low-level hardware programming.
- **Networking and Web Services**: Rust powers fast web frameworks like Actix and Rocket.
- **Cryptography and Security**: Many security-focused projects use Rust for its memory safety guarantees.

Comparing Rust to C and C++

Rust shares similarities with C and C++ but introduces major improvements:

Feature	C	C++	Rust
Memory Management	Manual (malloc/free)	Manual + RAII	Ownership/Borrowing
Safety	No built-in safety	Limited (smart pointers)	Enforced at compile time
Concurrency	Requires manual synchronization	Threading support	Fearless concurrency
Undefined Behavior	High risk	Medium risk	Eliminated by design
Compile-Time Checking	Limited	Better than C	Strict and enforced

A Simple Systems Programming Task in Rust

Let's compare a simple memory allocation example in Rust and C. This example dynamically allocates memory for an array.

C Example (Manual Memory Management)

```c
#include <stdio.h>
#include <stdlib.h>

int main() {
    int* arr = (int*)malloc(5 * sizeof(int));
    if (arr == NULL) {
```

```c
        printf("Memory allocation failed\n");
        return 1;
    }

    for (int i = 0; i < 5; i++) {
        arr[i] = i * 10;
        printf("%d ", arr[i]);
    }

    free(arr); // Manual deallocation required
    return 0;
}
```

Rust Example (Safe Memory Management)

```rust
fn main() {
    let arr = vec![0, 10, 20, 30, 40]; // Automatically allocated
and deallocated

    for num in &arr {
        println!("{}", num);
    }
} // Memory is automatically freed when 'arr' goes out of scope
```

Why Rust's Memory Management Matters

In Rust, there's no need for manual `malloc` or `free` calls. The ownership system ensures that memory is freed when it is no longer needed, preventing leaks and dangling pointers.

Key takeaways:

- Rust enforces memory safety at compile time.
- The borrow checker prevents invalid memory access.
- Developers don't have to manually track allocations and deallocations.

Rust's Growing Ecosystem

Rust is supported by a thriving ecosystem of libraries and tools, making it a practical choice for systems programming. Some notable projects using Rust include:

- **Mozilla's Servo**: A next-generation web rendering engine.
- **Dropbox**: Uses Rust for performance-critical services.

- **AWS Firecracker**: A lightweight virtualization tool built in Rust.
- **Microsoft Azure IoT Edge**: Uses Rust for secure cloud-edge computing.

Conclusion

Rust is revolutionizing systems programming by providing a safer alternative to C and C++ without sacrificing performance. Its ownership model, strict compiler checks, and modern concurrency primitives make it an ideal language for building reliable and efficient systems software.

As we proceed in this book, we will explore Rust's core concepts, from its ownership system to advanced features like async programming, macros, and WebAssembly integration. Whether you're a beginner or an experienced systems programmer, Rust provides a powerful and safe foundation for low-level programming.

Why Rust? Safety, Speed, and Concurrency

Rust has gained widespread adoption in systems programming due to its unique combination of **memory safety, performance, and concurrency**. Traditional systems languages like C and C++ offer low-level control but come with significant risks, such as memory corruption and data races. Rust addresses these problems while maintaining the efficiency required for high-performance applications.

This section explores why Rust stands out in the programming landscape, detailing how its core features make it a compelling choice for modern software development.

Memory Safety Without Garbage Collection

Memory safety is a critical concern in systems programming. Languages like C and C++ provide manual memory management, allowing fine-grained control but also leading to common pitfalls like **buffer overflows, use-after-free errors, and null pointer dereferencing**. Traditionally, memory-safe languages rely on **garbage collection (GC)**, but GC introduces runtime overhead, which is undesirable in performance-critical applications.

Rust introduces **memory safety without garbage collection** through its ownership system, which ensures:

- **Automatic memory management**: Memory is freed when it goes out of scope, eliminating leaks.
- **Compile-time checks**: Rust enforces strict rules to prevent unsafe memory access.
- **No runtime penalty**: Since Rust does not use a garbage collector, performance remains optimal.

Consider this C++ example where an object is manually allocated and deleted:

```
#include <iostream>
```

```cpp
class Example {
public:
    Example() { std::cout << "Constructor\n"; }
    ~Example() { std::cout << "Destructor\n"; }
};

int main() {
    Example* ex = new Example();
    delete ex; // Manual deallocation required
    return 0;
}
```

If the `delete` statement is forgotten, the program suffers from a **memory leak**. In contrast, Rust eliminates this issue using **ownership and automatic deallocation**:

```rust
struct Example;

impl Example {
    fn new() -> Self {
        println!("Constructor");
        Example
    }
}

fn main() {
    let ex = Example::new(); // No need for manual deallocation
} // Memory is automatically freed here
```

The Rust compiler ensures memory safety by enforcing **ownership rules**. A variable owns its memory, and when it goes out of scope, Rust automatically **deallocates** it. This prevents **double frees, use-after-free bugs, and memory leaks**.

Zero-Cost Abstractions for High Performance

Rust follows the philosophy of **zero-cost abstractions**, meaning high-level language features do not impose a performance cost compared to low-level code. The Rust compiler optimizes away abstractions, allowing developers to write **expressive code without sacrificing speed**.

Some examples of zero-cost abstractions in Rust include:

- **Iterators**: Rust's iterators compile down to efficient loops without overhead.

- **Traits and Generics**: Enable code reuse without runtime penalties.
- **Pattern Matching**: Optimized at compile-time for efficient execution.

Consider a simple Rust program that iterates over a list of numbers:

```rust
fn main() {
    let numbers = vec![1, 2, 3, 4, 5];

    let sum: i32 = numbers.iter().sum();
    println!("Sum: {}", sum);
}
```

Although this code appears high-level, Rust compiles it into efficient machine code comparable to a manually written loop.

Fearless Concurrency: Eliminating Data Races

Concurrency is essential for modern software but also introduces **race conditions, deadlocks, and undefined behavior** in languages like C and C++. Rust prevents these issues with a strict ownership system that ensures **thread safety at compile time**.

Rust achieves **fearless concurrency** through:

- **Ownership rules**: Prevents multiple mutable references to the same data.
- **Thread-safe primitives**: `Arc<T>` (Atomic Reference Counting) and `Mutex<T>` ensure safe shared state.
- **Async/Await**: Enables efficient non-blocking programming.

In C++, managing shared data across threads requires explicit locking mechanisms, which are prone to deadlocks:

```cpp
#include <iostream>
#include <thread>
#include <mutex>

std::mutex mtx;
int counter = 0;

void increment() {
    std::lock_guard<std::mutex> lock(mtx);
    counter++;
}
```

```cpp
int main() {
    std::thread t1(increment);
    std::thread t2(increment);

    t1.join();
    t2.join();

    std::cout << "Counter: " << counter << std::endl;
}
```

While this works, missing a `lock_guard` or unlocking manually can cause serious issues. Rust eliminates these risks:

```rust
use std::sync::{Arc, Mutex};
use std::thread;

fn main() {
    let counter = Arc::new(Mutex::new(0));

    let handles: Vec<_> = (0..2).map(|_| {
        let counter = Arc::clone(&counter);
        thread::spawn(move || {
            let mut num = counter.lock().unwrap();
            *num += 1;
        })
    }).collect();

    for handle in handles {
        handle.join().unwrap();
    }

    println!("Counter: {:?}", *counter.lock().unwrap());
}
```

Here, `Arc<T>` allows shared ownership of `Mutex<T>`, ensuring safe access across threads without data races.

Interoperability with C and Low-Level Programming

Rust is designed to be **compatible with C**, allowing developers to integrate Rust into existing systems. Rust's **Foreign Function Interface (FFI)** makes it easy to call C libraries while maintaining safety guarantees.

A simple Rust function callable from C:

```
#[no_mangle]
pub extern "C" fn add(a: i32, b: i32) -> i32 {
    a + b
}
```

This function can be linked and used in C:

```
#include <stdio.h>

extern int add(int a, int b);

int main() {
    printf("Sum: %d\n", add(3, 4));
    return 0;
}
```

By leveraging Rust for memory-safe operations while maintaining C compatibility, developers can gradually adopt Rust in **existing C-based projects**.

Modern Tooling and Developer Experience

Rust's tooling ecosystem improves **developer productivity**:

- **Cargo**: Rust's package manager and build system simplifies dependency management.
- **Rustfmt**: Ensures consistent code formatting.
- **Clippy**: A linting tool that provides helpful warnings and suggestions.
- **Rust Analyzer**: Provides powerful IDE support.

A new Rust project can be created with a single command:

```
cargo new my_project
```

Building and running the project is just as easy:

```
cargo build
cargo run
```

These tools make Rust development **fast, efficient, and enjoyable**.

Security: Preventing Common Vulnerabilities

Memory safety vulnerabilities, such as **buffer overflows and use-after-free errors**, are responsible for many security breaches. Rust's **strict compile-time checks** eliminate entire classes of security flaws.

For example, this C program can cause a **buffer overflow**:

```c
#include <stdio.h>
#include <string.h>

int main() {
    char buffer[10];
    strcpy(buffer, "This is too long!");
    printf("%s\n", buffer);
    return 0;
}
```

Rust prevents this at compile-time:

```rust
fn main() {
    let buffer = String::from("This is safe!");
    println!("{}", buffer);
}
```

Rust's safety mechanisms significantly **reduce attack surfaces** in security-critical applications.

Conclusion: Why Rust is the Future of Systems Programming

Rust provides an **unparalleled combination of safety, speed, and concurrency**. Unlike C and C++, Rust **eliminates memory bugs at compile time** without sacrificing performance. With its **modern concurrency model, powerful tooling, and secure design**, Rust is becoming the preferred choice for:

- **Operating systems** (Linux kernel, Redox OS)

- **Embedded systems** (IoT and real-time applications)
- **Networking and web services** (Tokio, Actix)
- **Security-critical software** (cryptography, blockchain)

By embracing Rust, developers can build reliable, high-performance software **without the risks traditionally associated with systems programming**. The rest of this book will explore Rust's features in depth, demonstrating how it can be effectively used to create robust and efficient applications.

Setting Up Your Rust Development Environment

Setting up a proper development environment is the first step toward writing efficient and reliable Rust programs. This section will guide you through installing Rust, configuring your development tools, understanding Rust's package manager, and setting up an integrated development environment (IDE) for a seamless coding experience.

Installing Rust

The official way to install Rust is through `rustup`, a command-line tool that manages Rust versions and components. `rustup` ensures that you always have the latest stable version of Rust while also allowing you to switch between different versions if needed.

Installing Rust on Windows, macOS, and Linux

To install Rust, open a terminal and run:

```
curl --proto '=https' --tlsv1.2 -sSf https://sh.rustup.rs | sh
```

This command downloads and runs the official Rust installer. You will be prompted to confirm the installation. Once installed, restart your terminal or run:

```
source $HOME/.cargo/env
```

To verify that Rust is installed, use:

```
rustc --version
```

This should display the installed Rust version:

```
rustc 1.x.x (yyyy-mm-dd)
```

Using Rust on Windows

For Windows users, Rust can be installed using **Rustup**. The recommended way is to install the Windows Subsystem for Linux (WSL) for a more Unix-like development environment, but Rust also works natively on Windows.

To install Rust on Windows:

1. Download and run the Rustup installer from https://rustup.rs.
2. Follow the installation instructions.
3. Ensure that Rust is added to your system's PATH by restarting your terminal.

Updating and Uninstalling Rust

Rust is frequently updated, so it's a good practice to keep your installation up to date. Run:

```
rustup update
```

If you need to uninstall Rust, use:

```
rustup self uninstall
```

Understanding Cargo: Rust's Package Manager

Cargo is Rust's official package manager and build system. It simplifies dependency management, compilation, and project organization. Cargo is installed automatically with Rust.

To verify Cargo's installation, run:

```
cargo --version
```

Cargo allows you to:

- **Create new projects**
- **Manage dependencies**
- **Compile Rust code**
- **Run tests**
- **Build and publish Rust libraries**

Creating a New Rust Project

To start a new Rust project, use:

```
cargo new my_project
cd my_project
```

This creates the following directory structure:

```
my_project
|── Cargo.toml
└── src
    └── main.rs
```

- `Cargo.toml`: Defines the project's metadata and dependencies.
- `src/main.rs`: Contains the main program entry point.

To build and run the project, execute:

```
cargo run
```

Cargo automatically fetches dependencies, compiles the code, and runs the program.

Adding Dependencies with Cargo

Rust projects often rely on external libraries (crates). To add a dependency, open `Cargo.toml` and include:

```
[dependencies]
serde = "1.0"
```

Then, run:

```
cargo build
```

Cargo fetches and compiles `serde`, making it available for use in your Rust program.

Choosing a Rust IDE and Editor

An efficient IDE or editor enhances productivity. Here are the most commonly used editors for Rust:

VS Code (Recommended)

Visual Studio Code (VS Code) is one of the best editors for Rust due to its extensive support for extensions and debugging.

Setting up Rust in VS Code:

1. Install Visual Studio Code.
2. Install the **Rust Analyzer** extension from the VS Code marketplace.
3. Open your Rust project in VS Code.

Rust Analyzer provides:

- Autocompletion
- Syntax highlighting
- Type inference
- Inline error checking

JetBrains CLion

CLion is a powerful IDE for Rust development, providing deep code analysis and an integrated debugger.

Setting up Rust in CLion:

1. Install CLion.
2. Install the Rust plugin via **Settings → Plugins**.
3. Open your Rust project.

Neovim and Vim

For developers who prefer terminal-based editors, Neovim and Vim offer lightweight alternatives.

To configure Rust support in Neovim:

1. Install the `rust-analyzer` language server.
2. Use the `coc.nvim` or `nvim-lspconfig` plugin for autocompletion.
3. Configure Neovim's `init.vim` or `init.lua` to enable Rust integration.

Other Editors

- **Sublime Text**: Requires Rust syntax highlighting and the Rust Analyzer package.
- **Emacs**: Supports Rust through `rust-mode` and `lsp-mode`.

Setting Up Debugging for Rust

Debugging is an essential part of development. The best way to debug Rust programs is using **LLDB** or **GDB**.

Debugging with GDB

Install GDB:

```
sudo apt install gdb
```

Compile the Rust program with debug symbols:

```
cargo build --debug
```

Run the program inside GDB:

```
gdb target/debug/my_project
```

Debugging with VS Code

1. Install the **CodeLLDB** extension.
2. Open the Rust project.
3. Add a **launch.json** configuration for debugging:

```
{
    "version": "0.2.0",
    "configurations": [
        {
            "name": "Debug Rust",
            "type": "lldb",
            "request": "launch",
            "program": "${workspaceFolder}/target/debug/my_project",
            "cwd": "${workspaceFolder}"
        }
    ]
}
```

4. Press **F5** to start debugging.

Configuring Rust for Cross-Compilation

Rust supports **cross-compilation**, allowing you to build applications for different target architectures.

To list available targets:

```
rustc --print target-list
```

To compile for a specific target:

```
rustup target add x86_64-unknown-linux-gnu
cargo build --target=x86_64-unknown-linux-gnu
```

This is useful for embedded development, ARM architectures, and Windows/Linux cross-compilation.

Version Control with Git and Rust

Using Git with Rust ensures better project management. To initialize a Rust project with Git:

```
git init
git add .
git commit -m "Initial commit"
```

To add a `.gitignore` file for Rust:

```
target/
Cargo.lock
```

Setting Up Rust Formatting and Linting

Rust provides built-in tools for formatting and linting:

- **Rustfmt**: Formats Rust code consistently.

```
rustfmt src/main.rs
```

To automatically format all files:

```
cargo fmt
```

- **Clippy**: A linting tool that catches potential issues.

```
cargo clippy
```

Clippy helps improve code quality by suggesting optimizations and best practices.

Testing Rust Code

Rust has built-in support for unit testing. To add a test, create a `tests` module inside `src/main.rs`:

```
#[cfg(test)]
mod tests {
    #[test]
    fn it_works() {
        assert_eq!(2 + 2, 4);
    }
}
```

Run tests with:

```
cargo test
```

Rust will execute all test cases and display the results.

Conclusion

Setting up a proper Rust development environment is crucial for efficient programming. By installing Rust with `rustup`, using Cargo for package management, choosing a suitable editor, configuring debugging tools, and setting up Git, developers can streamline their workflow. As you continue to develop Rust applications, these tools and techniques will enhance your productivity and code quality.

Your First Rust Program: Hello, World!

Writing your first Rust program is a crucial step in understanding how Rust works. This section will guide you through creating, compiling, and running a simple Rust program. We will also explore key concepts such as the Rust execution model, project structure, error handling, and debugging.

Writing "Hello, World!" in Rust

Rust follows a straightforward syntax for its basic programs. The classic "Hello, World!" program looks like this:

```rust
fn main() {
    println!("Hello, World!");
}
```

Breaking Down the Code

- `fn main() {}`: Defines the `main` function, which serves as the entry point of every Rust program.
- `println!("Hello, World!");`: The `println!` macro prints the text to the console. The exclamation mark (`!`) indicates that `println!` is a macro rather than a function.

Compiling and Running the Program

To execute this program, follow these steps:

Create a new Rust project using Cargo:

sh

```sh
cargo new hello_rust
cd hello_rust
```

1. This creates a directory named `hello_rust` with a preconfigured Rust project.

Open `src/main.rs` and modify it:

rust

```rust
fn main() {
    println!("Hello, Rust!");
}
```

2.

Build and run the project:

sh

```
cargo run
```
You should see:

```
Hello, Rust!
```

    3.

Alternatively, to compile the program without running it:

```
cargo build
```

This generates an executable inside the `target/debug/` directory, which can be run manually:

```
./target/debug/hello_rust
```

Understanding Rust's Compilation Model

Rust is a **compiled** language, meaning source code is translated into machine code before execution. This differs from **interpreted** languages like Python, where code is executed line-by-line.

When you run `cargo build`, Rust's compiler (`rustc`) performs:

1. **Lexical Analysis**: Converts source code into tokens.
2. **Parsing**: Checks syntax and generates an abstract syntax tree (AST).
3. **Ownership and Borrowing Checks**: Ensures memory safety.
4. **Intermediate Representation (MIR & LLVM IR)**: Converts Rust code into an optimized low-level format.
5. **Machine Code Generation**: Produces the final executable.

This compilation pipeline ensures Rust programs are **fast and safe**, with aggressive optimizations.

Exploring the Cargo Project Structure

A Rust project created with `cargo new` has the following structure:

```
hello_rust/
|— Cargo.toml  # Project metadata and dependencies
```

```
| — src/
|   | — main.rs  # Main source file
| — target/  # Compiled output (generated after build)
```

`Cargo.toml` is the project's configuration file. It defines dependencies and metadata:

toml

```toml
[package]
name = "hello_rust"
version = "0.1.0"
edition = "2021"

[dependencies]
```

-
- `src/main.rs` contains the actual Rust code.

- The `target/` directory is automatically generated and holds compiled binaries.

To clean the project and remove compiled artifacts:

```
cargo clean
```

Handling User Input in Rust

A useful enhancement to the "Hello, World!" program is allowing user input. Rust provides the `std::io` module for reading input:

```rust
use std::io;

fn main() {
    let mut name = String::new();

    println!("Enter your name: ");
    io::stdin().read_line(&mut name).expect("Failed to read input");

    println!("Hello, {}!", name.trim());
}
```

Understanding the Code

- `let mut name = String::new();`: Creates a mutable `String` to store user input.
- `io::stdin().read_line(&mut name)`: Reads a line from the terminal and stores it in `name`.
- `.trim()`: Removes trailing newline characters from input.

Understanding Variables and Mutability in Rust

Rust enforces immutability by default. The following code will **not** compile:

```rust
fn main() {
    let name = "Alice";
    name = "Bob"; // Error: cannot assign twice to immutable
variable
}
```

To allow modification, use the `mut` keyword:

```rust
fn main() {
    let mut name = String::from("Alice");
    name.push_str(" Bob");
    println!("{}", name);
}
```

Error Handling in Rust

Rust's error handling is based on the `Result` and `Option` types. Let's modify our input-handling example to catch potential errors:

```rust
use std::io;

fn main() {
    println!("Enter your name:");

    let mut name = String::new();
    match io::stdin().read_line(&mut name) {
        Ok(_) => println!("Hello, {}!", name.trim()),
        Err(e) => println!("Error: {}", e),
```

```
    }
}
```

Here, `read_line()` returns a `Result` type:

- `Ok(_)`: Runs if the input is successful.
- `Err(e)`: Captures and prints an error message.

Debugging Your First Rust Program

Rust includes powerful debugging tools. Consider this code:

```
fn main() {
    let numbers = vec![1, 2, 3];
    println!("{}", numbers[3]); // Error: Index out of bounds
}
```

Running this results in:

```
thread 'main' panicked at 'index out of bounds: the len is 3 but the
index is 3'
```

Rust prevents out-of-bounds errors at runtime by checking array sizes.

Using Debug Mode

Rust allows debug printing with `dbg!`:

```
fn main() {
    let num = 10;
    dbg!(num);
}
```

The output includes file and line information:

```
[src/main.rs:3] num = 10
```

To enable detailed debug info, compile with:

```
cargo build --debug
```

Formatting Rust Code with `rustfmt`

Rust provides an automatic formatter:

```
cargo fmt
```

This ensures consistent styling across projects.

Compiling Rust for Different Targets

Rust supports cross-compilation for different operating systems. To compile for Windows on Linux:

```
rustup target add x86_64-pc-windows-gnu
cargo build --target=x86_64-pc-windows-gnu
```

This produces a Windows-compatible executable.

Optimizing Performance with `cargo build --release`

Rust builds in **debug mode** by default, adding extra checks. For optimized binaries, use:

```
cargo build --release
```

This significantly reduces binary size and improves execution speed.

Conclusion

This section introduced Rust's basic syntax, compilation process, project structure, error handling, debugging, and performance optimizations. By setting up a Rust project, writing a simple "Hello, World!" program, handling user input, and using Cargo, you now have a strong foundation to build more complex Rust applications. The next chapter will dive deeper into Rust's core concepts, including variables, ownership, and control flow.

Chapter 2: Rust Fundamentals: The Building Blocks

Variables, Constants, and Data Types

Rust is a statically typed language, which means that all variables must have a defined type at compile time. However, Rust also provides type inference, so you don't always have to explicitly annotate types. In this section, we will explore variables, constants, and data types in Rust.

Variables in Rust

In Rust, variables are declared using the `let` keyword:

```
fn main() {
    let x = 5; // Immutable variable
    println!("The value of x is: {}", x);
}
```

By default, Rust variables are immutable, meaning their values cannot be changed after assignment. This immutability enforces safety by preventing accidental modifications.

To make a variable mutable, use the `mut` keyword:

```
fn main() {
    let mut x = 5;
    println!("Before mutation: {}", x);
    x = 10;
    println!("After mutation: {}", x);
}
```

This allows x to be reassigned a new value.

Constants in Rust

Constants in Rust are declared using the `const` keyword and must always have an explicitly defined type. Unlike variables, constants cannot be mutable.

```
const MAX_SCORE: u32 = 100_000;
```

```
fn main() {
    println!("The maximum score is: {}", MAX_SCORE);
}
```

Constants are typically used for values that are known at compile time and will not change throughout the execution of the program.

Shadowing

Rust allows variable shadowing, which means a new variable with the same name can be declared in the same scope, effectively replacing the previous one:

```
fn main() {
    let x = 5;
    let x = x + 1; // Shadowing the previous x
    let x = x * 2;

    println!("The value of x is: {}", x);
}
```

Shadowing is different from mutability because the new variable can have a different type.

Data Types in Rust

Rust has a strong type system that ensures memory safety and performance. The data types in Rust are categorized into scalar and compound types.

Scalar Types

Rust's scalar types represent single values. These include integers, floating-point numbers, Booleans, and characters.

- **Integer Types**: Rust supports signed (i8, i16, i32, i64, i128, isize) and unsigned (u8, u16, u32, u64, u128, usize) integers.
- **Floating-Point Types**: f32 and f64 represent 32-bit and 64-bit floating-point numbers, respectively.
- **Boolean Type**: bool represents a Boolean value, either true or false.
- **Character Type**: char represents a single Unicode character.

Example:

```
fn main() {
```

```
    let int_value: i32 = -42;
    let float_value: f64 = 3.14;
    let is_rust_fun: bool = true;
    let letter: char = 'R';

    println!("Integer: {}, Float: {}, Boolean: {}, Char: {}",
int_value, float_value, is_rust_fun, letter);
}
```

Compound Types

Rust provides two primary compound types: tuples and arrays.

- **Tuples**: A tuple is a fixed-size collection of values of different types.

```
fn main() {
    let person: (&str, i32, f64) = ("Alice", 30, 68.5);
    println!("Name: {}, Age: {}, Weight: {}", person.0, person.1,
person.2);
}
```

- **Arrays**: Arrays contain multiple values of the same type.

```
fn main() {
    let numbers: [i32; 4] = [1, 2, 3, 4];
    println!("First number: {}", numbers[0]);
}
```

Type Inference

Rust can automatically determine the type of a variable based on the value assigned:

```
fn main() {
    let number = 42; // Rust infers i32
    let decimal = 4.2; // Rust infers f64

    println!("Number: {}, Decimal: {}", number, decimal);
}
```

Explicit type annotations are useful when the type is ambiguous or when working with APIs that expect specific types.

Type Conversion

Rust does not allow implicit type conversions to prevent unintended data loss. Instead, explicit conversion must be performed using the `as` keyword:

```rust
fn main() {
    let x: i32 = 5;
    let y: f64 = x as f64 / 2.0; // Explicit conversion

    println!("Converted value: {}", y);
}
```

Constants vs. Immutable Variables

Feature	Constants (`const`)	Immutable Variables (`let`)
Mutability	Always immutable	Immutable by default, can be made mutable
Scope	Global and function scope	Limited to the scope they are declared in
Type Annotation	Required	Optional
Reassignment	Not allowed	Shadowing allows reassignment

Summary

- Variables are immutable by default; use `mut` for mutability.
- Constants are always immutable and must have explicit types.
- Shadowing allows redeclaring variables within the same scope.
- Rust's strong type system ensures safety through explicit data types.
- Scalar types include integers, floating-point numbers, Booleans, and characters.
- Compound types include tuples and arrays.
- Type inference helps reduce verbosity but explicit types are sometimes necessary.
- Rust enforces explicit type conversion to prevent unintended behavior.

By mastering Rust's variable system and data types, you lay the groundwork for understanding ownership, borrowing, and memory safety, which are core features of Rust's design philosophy.

Ownership, Borrowing, and Lifetimes

Rust's memory management model is one of its most defining features. Unlike languages that use garbage collection (such as Java or Python) or manual memory management (such as C or C++), Rust employs a unique ownership system that ensures memory safety without a garbage collector. This system revolves around three key principles: **ownership, borrowing, and lifetimes**.

Mastering these concepts is crucial to writing safe and efficient Rust programs. In this section, we will explore these concepts in detail and understand how they work through practical examples.

Ownership in Rust

Rust's ownership system ensures that each piece of memory has a single owner at any given time. When an owner goes out of scope, Rust automatically deallocates the memory, preventing issues such as memory leaks and dangling pointers.

Rules of Ownership

1. Each value in Rust has a single owner.
2. When the owner goes out of scope, the value is dropped (freed from memory).
3. Ownership can be transferred to another variable.

Let's examine ownership in practice:

```
fn main() {
    let s = String::from("Hello, Rust!"); // s is the owner of the
string
    takes_ownership(s); // Ownership moves to the function
    // println!("{}", s); // This would cause an error since s is no
longer valid

    let x = 42; // x is an integer
    makes_copy(x); // Since i32 implements the Copy trait, x is
still valid after this
    println!("{}", x); // No error, x was copied, not moved
}

fn takes_ownership(some_string: String) {
    println!("{}", some_string);
} // some_string goes out of scope and memory is freed

fn makes_copy(some_integer: i32) {
```

```
    println!("{}", some_integer);
} // some_integer goes out of scope but nothing is freed
```

Move Semantics

Rust enforces **move semantics** when working with heap-allocated data such as `String`. When an assignment occurs, the ownership is transferred, and the original owner is no longer valid.

```
fn main() {
    let s1 = String::from("Rust");
    let s2 = s1; // s1 is moved to s2

    // println!("{}", s1); // Error! s1 is no longer valid
    println!("{}", s2);
}
```

Unlike primitive types (e.g., integers, floats, booleans), which implement the **Copy trait**, heap-allocated types like `String` do not implement `Copy` by default. Instead, they are moved when assigned to another variable.

Clone for Deep Copies

To create a deep copy instead of moving ownership, Rust provides the `clone()` method.

```
fn main() {
    let s1 = String::from("Rust");
    let s2 = s1.clone(); // Creates a deep copy

    println!("s1: {}, s2: {}", s1, s2); // Both are valid
}
```

Using `clone()` ensures that the original value remains accessible after assignment.

Borrowing in Rust

While ownership prevents data races and memory issues, it can be restrictive. Borrowing allows functions to access a value **without taking ownership**.

Rust achieves this through **references**, which let multiple parts of the code access a variable without transferring ownership.

Immutable Borrowing

An immutable borrow allows a function to read data without modifying it. The syntax uses the & operator.

```
fn main() {
    let s = String::from("Rust");
    print_length(&s); // Borrowing s, ownership not transferred
    println!("String is still valid: {}", s);
}

fn print_length(s: &String) {
    println!("Length: {}", s.len());
}
```

Mutable Borrowing

A mutable borrow allows a function to modify the borrowed value. However, **Rust enforces a strict rule: only one mutable borrow is allowed at a time** to prevent data races.

```
fn main() {
    let mut s = String::from("Hello");
    change(&mut s);
    println!("Modified string: {}", s);
}

fn change(some_string: &mut String) {
    some_string.push_str(", Rust!");
}
```

Borrowing Rules

1. Any number of immutable references (&T) can exist simultaneously.
2. Only **one** mutable reference (&mut T) is allowed at a time.
3. Immutable and mutable references **cannot coexist**.

Example of an error:

```
fn main() {
    let mut s = String::from("Rust");

    let r1 = &s; // Immutable borrow
    let r2 = &s; // Another immutable borrow

    // let r3 = &mut s; // Error! Cannot have a mutable borrow while
immutable borrows exist
    println!("{}, {}", r1, r2);
}
```

Once the immutable references are no longer used, a mutable borrow can be introduced.

Lifetimes in Rust

Lifetimes ensure that references remain valid for the necessary duration. While Rust's ownership and borrowing rules prevent issues like dangling pointers, lifetimes explicitly define how long references should be valid.

The Problem of Dangling References

A dangling reference occurs when a reference points to a value that has been deallocated.

```
fn dangle() -> &String {
    let s = String::from("Rust");
    &s // Error! s is dropped when function ends
}
```

Rust prevents this at compile time.

Explicit Lifetimes

Rust requires explicit lifetimes when returning references from functions to ensure that the referenced value lives long enough.

```
fn longest<'a>(s1: &'a str, s2: &'a str) -> &'a str {
    if s1.len() > s2.len() {
        s1
    } else {
        s2
```

```
    }
}

fn main() {
    let string1 = String::from("Rust");
    let string2 = String::from("Programming");

    let result = longest(&string1, &string2);
    println!("The longest string is: {}", result);
}
```

Understanding 'a

- The 'a lifetime annotation means that both input references (s1, s2) and the output reference (&str) **must have the same lifetime**.
- Rust guarantees that the returned reference remains valid as long as the shortest-lived input reference.

Structs with Lifetimes

When a struct contains references, lifetimes must be declared explicitly:

```
struct Important<'a> {
    content: &'a str,
}

fn main() {
    let text = String::from("Rust is awesome!");
    let imp = Important { content: &text };

    println!("{}", imp.content);
}
```

Summary

- **Ownership** ensures that each value has a single owner.
- **Move semantics** prevent double-free errors.
- **Borrowing** allows references to data without transferring ownership.
- **Mutable borrowing** allows modification but enforces exclusivity.
- **Lifetimes** prevent dangling references and enforce reference validity.

Mastering ownership, borrowing, and lifetimes is key to writing efficient and safe Rust programs. By adhering to Rust's memory safety model, developers can write concurrent, high-performance applications without encountering common pitfalls like null pointer dereferences and data races.

Structs, Enums, and Pattern Matching

Rust provides powerful ways to define custom data structures using **structs** and **enums**. These features enable developers to build expressive and type-safe applications. Additionally, Rust's **pattern matching** system allows for concise and readable control flow, making it a core part of idiomatic Rust programming.

Structs in Rust

A **struct** in Rust is a collection of related data grouped together. Structs are useful for representing complex data types.

Defining and Using Structs

A basic struct definition looks like this:

```rust
struct User {
    username: String,
    email: String,
    age: u32,
}

fn main() {
    let user1 = User {
        username: String::from("alice"),
        email: String::from("alice@example.com"),
        age: 25,
    };

    println!("User: {} ({})", user1.username, user1.age);
}
```

Each field in a struct has a name and a type. The values must be explicitly set when creating an instance.

Structs with Mutable Fields

To modify a field in a struct, the instance must be mutable:

```
fn main() {
    let mut user = User {
        username: String::from("bob"),
        email: String::from("bob@example.com"),
        age: 30,
    };

    user.age += 1;
    println!("Updated age: {}", user.age);
}
```

Struct Update Syntax

Rust allows struct updates using the `..` syntax, which copies remaining fields from another instance:

```
fn main() {
    let user1 = User {
        username: String::from("charlie"),
        email: String::from("charlie@example.com"),
        age: 28,
    };

    let user2 = User {
        email: String::from("charlie_new@example.com"),
        ..user1
    };

    println!("User2 Email: {}", user2.email);
}
```

However, `user1` is no longer valid after this if it contains heap-allocated fields like `String`, as ownership of the remaining fields is moved.

Tuple Structs

Tuple structs are a variation that allows defining structs without named fields:

```
struct Point(i32, i32);

fn main() {
    let p1 = Point(10, 20);
    println!("Point: ({}, {})", p1.0, p1.1);
}
```

These are useful for grouping related values without needing explicit names.

Methods on Structs

Methods in Rust are defined within an `impl` (implementation) block:

```
struct Rectangle {
    width: u32,
    height: u32,
}

impl Rectangle {
    fn area(&self) -> u32 {
        self.width * self.height
    }
}

fn main() {
    let rect = Rectangle { width: 30, height: 50 };
    println!("Area: {}", rect.area());
}
```

The `self` parameter represents the instance the method is called on.

Enums in Rust

Enums allow defining a type that can have multiple variants, each potentially holding different data.

Defining and Using Enums

```rust
enum IpAddr {
    V4(String),
    V6(String),
}

fn main() {
    let home = IpAddr::V4(String::from("127.0.0.1"));
    let loopback = IpAddr::V6(String::from("::1"));

    match home {
        IpAddr::V4(addr) => println!("IPv4: {}", addr),
        IpAddr::V6(addr) => println!("IPv6: {}", addr),
    }
}
```

Each variant can hold different types of data.

The Option Enum

Rust's Option<T> enum represents an optional value:

```rust
fn divide(numerator: f64, denominator: f64) -> Option<f64> {
    if denominator == 0.0 {
        None
    } else {
        Some(numerator / denominator)
    }
}

fn main() {
    let result = divide(10.0, 2.0);
    match result {
        Some(value) => println!("Result: {}", value),
        None => println!("Cannot divide by zero!"),
    }
}
```

Rust does not have null, but Option<T> serves the same purpose safely.

Pattern Matching

Pattern matching in Rust is done using the `match` keyword. It provides an elegant way to work with enums, structs, and even primitive types.

Match with Enums

```rust
enum Coin {
    Penny,
    Nickel,
    Dime,
    Quarter,
}

fn coin_value(coin: Coin) -> u32 {
    match coin {
        Coin::Penny => 1,
        Coin::Nickel => 5,
        Coin::Dime => 10,
        Coin::Quarter => 25,
    }
}

fn main() {
    let coin = Coin::Dime;
    println!("Value: {} cents", coin_value(coin));
}
```

Each match arm corresponds to a possible value of the enum.

Match with Structs

Pattern matching can also destructure structs:

```rust
struct Point {
    x: i32,
    y: i32,
}

fn main() {
    let p = Point { x: 10, y: 20 };
```

```
    match p {
        Point { x, y: 0 } => println!("Point on x-axis: {}", x),
        Point { x: 0, y } => println!("Point on y-axis: {}", y),
        Point { x, y } => println!("Point at ({}, {})", x, y),
    }
}
```

Using _ as a Catch-All Pattern

If some cases do not require specific handling, _ can be used:

```
fn main() {
    let number = 5;

    match number {
        1 => println!("One"),
        2 | 3 => println!("Two or Three"),
        _ => println!("Some other number"),
    }
}
```

The if let and while let Expressions

For simple match cases, if let provides a more concise syntax:

```
fn main() {
    let some_value = Some(10);

    if let Some(x) = some_value {
        println!("Found: {}", x);
    }
}
```

while let is used in loops:

```
fn main() {
    let mut numbers = vec![1, 2, 3];
```

```
while let Some(num) = numbers.pop() {
    println!("Popped: {}", num);
}
}
```

Summary

- **Structs** group related data and can have methods.
- **Tuple structs** are unnamed field structs.
- **Enums** define a type that can have multiple variants.
- **Pattern matching** enables concise control flow for working with data.
- The `match` **statement** handles different variants in an expressive way.
- The `if let` **and** `while let` **expressions** simplify cases where only one variant matters.

By combining structs, enums, and pattern matching, Rust allows writing expressive and safe code that enforces strong type guarantees. These features help build applications that are both reliable and easy to maintain.

Functions and Control Flow

Functions and control flow structures form the backbone of Rust programming, enabling code reuse, organization, and decision-making. Rust's function system is both expressive and efficient, ensuring that developers can write clean, safe, and performant code.

Defining and Calling Functions

Rust functions are declared using the `fn` keyword. They can take parameters and return values.

Basic Function Syntax

```
fn greet(name: &str) {
    println!("Hello, {}!", name);
}

fn main() {
    greet("Alice");
}
```

This function takes a string slice (&str) as an argument and prints a greeting message.

Function Parameters and Return Values

Rust functions can take multiple parameters and return values.

```
fn add(a: i32, b: i32) -> i32 {
    a + b // No semicolon indicates an implicit return
}

fn main() {
    let result = add(5, 10);
    println!("Sum: {}", result);
}
```

- The -> i32 specifies the return type.
- Rust functions return the last expression implicitly if there is no return keyword.

Explicit Return Statements

```
fn multiply(a: i32, b: i32) -> i32 {
    return a * b; // Explicit return
}
```

Expressions vs. Statements

Rust distinguishes between **statements** and **expressions**:

- **Statements** perform an action but do not return a value.
- **Expressions** evaluate to a value.

```
fn main() {
    let x = 5; // Statement
    let y = {
        let z = 3;
        z + 1 // Expression
    };
```

```
    println!("y is {}", y);
}
```

Blocks enclosed in {} are expressions when they return a value.

Conditional Control Flow: `if`

Rust provides `if` expressions for branching logic.

Basic `if` Statement

```
fn main() {
    let number = 10;

    if number > 5 {
        println!("The number is greater than 5");
    } else {
        println!("The number is 5 or less");
    }
}
```

`if` as an Expression

Since `if` is an expression, it can return a value:

```
fn main() {
    let condition = true;
    let number = if condition { 10 } else { 5 }; // Returns one of
two values
    println!("Number is: {}", number);
}
```

All branches must return the same type.

Looping Constructs

Rust provides three looping constructs: `loop`, `while`, and `for`.

Infinite Loops with `loop`

The `loop` keyword creates an infinite loop that must be exited manually.

```
fn main() {
    let mut count = 0;

    loop {
        count += 1;
        println!("Iteration {}", count);

        if count == 5 {
            break;
        }
    }
}
```

- `break` exits the loop.
- `continue` skips the rest of the iteration.

Returning Values from Loops

```
fn main() {
    let mut counter = 0;

    let result = loop {
        counter += 1;
        if counter == 10 {
            break counter * 2;
        }
    };

    println!("Loop result: {}", result);
}
```

The loop's result is assigned to `result`.

Conditional Loops with `while`

A `while` loop runs as long as its condition is `true`.

```rust
fn main() {
    let mut number = 3;

    while number > 0 {
        println!("{}!", number);
        number -= 1;
    }

    println!("Liftoff!");
}
```

Iterating with `for`

The `for` loop iterates over collections.

```rust
fn main() {
    let numbers = [1, 2, 3, 4, 5];

    for num in numbers.iter() {
        println!("Number: {}", num);
    }
}
```

Using `for` with Ranges

```rust
fn main() {
    for i in 1..5 {
        println!("{}", i); // Prints 1 to 4
    }

    for i in (1..5).rev() {
        println!("Countdown: {}", i);
    }
}
```

`match` as a Control Flow Construct

Rust's `match` statement is a powerful alternative to `if` statements.

```rust
fn main() {
    let number = 2;

    match number {
        1 => println!("One"),
        2 => println!("Two"),
        3 => println!("Three"),
        _ => println!("Something else"),
    }
}
```

- `_` acts as a wildcard to match anything.

Matching with Ranges

```rust
fn main() {
    let x = 7;

    match x {
        1..=5 => println!("Between 1 and 5"),
        6..=10 => println!("Between 6 and 10"),
        _ => println!("Outside range"),
    }
}
```

The `while let` Expression

`while let` continues looping while a pattern matches.

```rust
fn main() {
    let mut numbers = vec![1, 2, 3];

    while let Some(num) = numbers.pop() {
        println!("Popped: {}", num);
    }
```

```
}
```

The if let Expression

if let is used for concise pattern matching.

```rust
fn main() {
    let some_value = Some(10);

    if let Some(x) = some_value {
        println!("Found: {}", x);
    }
}
```

Error Handling with Result

Rust's Result type helps handle errors.

```rust
fn divide(numerator: f64, denominator: f64) -> Result<f64, String> {
    if denominator == 0.0 {
        Err(String::from("Cannot divide by zero"))
    } else {
        Ok(numerator / denominator)
    }
}

fn main() {
    let result = divide(10.0, 2.0);

    match result {
        Ok(value) => println!("Result: {}", value),
        Err(error) => println!("Error: {}", error),
    }
}
```

Summary

- **Functions** use `fn` and can return values implicitly.
- **Control flow** is handled with `if`, `match`, and loops.
- `loop` creates infinite loops; `while` loops until a condition is met.
- `for` **loops** iterate over collections and ranges.
- **Pattern matching** via `match`, `if let`, and `while let` simplifies control flow.
- **Error handling** with `Result<T, E>` prevents crashes.

By mastering functions and control flow, Rust developers can write robust, safe, and efficient code. These constructs form the foundation of any Rust program, ensuring smooth execution and decision-making capabilities.

Chapter 3: Memory Management in Rust

Stack vs. Heap Memory

Memory management is a fundamental aspect of systems programming, and Rust introduces unique concepts to ensure safety and efficiency. Unlike languages with garbage collection, Rust enforces memory safety at compile time through ownership and borrowing rules. To fully grasp how Rust manages memory, it's essential to understand the distinction between stack and heap memory.

Understanding Stack Memory

The stack is a region of memory that operates in a last-in, first-out (LIFO) manner. When a function is called, its local variables, including primitive types and references, are pushed onto the stack. Once the function execution completes, these variables are popped off the stack, making stack allocation highly efficient.

Characteristics of stack memory:

- **Fast allocation and deallocation:** Memory is allocated and freed automatically as functions are called and return.
- **Predictable memory access:** The order of allocation and deallocation is strictly maintained.
- **Limited size:** The stack is typically much smaller than the heap, making it unsuitable for storing large data structures.

Consider the following Rust code that demonstrates stack allocation:

```rust
fn main() {
    let x: i32 = 42; // Allocated on the stack
    let y: f64 = 3.14; // Also allocated on the stack

    println!("x: {}, y: {}", x, y);
}
```

In this example, both x and y are primitive types with a known, fixed size at compile time. They are stored directly on the stack and automatically cleaned up when the function exits.

Understanding Heap Memory

The heap is a larger and more flexible memory region used for dynamically allocated data. Unlike stack memory, which follows a strict LIFO order, heap allocation is managed at runtime. This makes heap allocations slightly slower than stack allocations.

Characteristics of heap memory:

- **Flexible size:** The heap can store large or dynamically sized data structures.
- **Manually managed:** Rust enforces strict ownership and borrowing rules to ensure memory safety without a garbage collector.
- **Slower access:** Accessing heap memory requires an additional pointer dereference, which adds a small performance overhead.

The following Rust example demonstrates heap allocation using `Box<T>`:

```
fn main() {
    let heap_value = Box::new(100); // Allocated on the heap

    println!("Heap value: {}", heap_value);
} // heap_value is automatically freed here
```

Here, `Box::new(100)` places the integer `100` on the heap, while `heap_value` itself (a pointer to the heap-allocated data) remains on the stack. When `heap_value` goes out of scope, Rust automatically deallocates the memory.

When to Use Stack vs. Heap

Feature	Stack Memory	Heap Memory
Speed	Fast	Slower due to allocation overhead
Size Limit	Small	Large, can grow dynamically
Ownership	Auto-managed	Requires explicit ownership
Data Type	Fixed-size types	Dynamically sized types

Use stack memory for simple, small, and short-lived data. Use heap memory for larger, dynamically sized, or long-lived data structures.

Heap Allocation and Dynamic Data Structures

Dynamic data structures like `Vec<T>`, `String`, and `HashMap<K, V>` rely on heap allocation. Consider the following example with a `Vec<i32>`:

```
fn main() {
```

```
    let mut numbers: Vec<i32> = Vec::new(); // Allocates on the heap
    numbers.push(10);
    numbers.push(20);
    numbers.push(30);

    println!("{:?}", numbers);
} // numbers is freed here
```

Although numbers itself is stored on the stack, its elements reside on the heap. When numbers goes out of scope, Rust automatically deallocates the associated heap memory.

Understanding Ownership in Rust

Rust enforces strict memory safety through ownership, ensuring that each value has a single owner. Consider this example:

```
fn main() {
    let s1 = String::from("hello"); // Allocated on the heap
    let s2 = s1; // s1 is moved to s2

    // println!("{}", s1); // This line would cause a compilation
error
}
```

Here, s1 is moved to s2, meaning s1 is no longer valid. This prevents double free errors and ensures that memory is properly managed.

Avoiding Memory Leaks in Rust

Although Rust prevents common memory safety issues, memory leaks can still occur when references are not properly released. One common cause is reference cycles in Rc<T> (reference counting smart pointers):

```
use std::rc::Rc;
use std::cell::RefCell;

struct Node {
    value: i32,
    next: Option<Rc<RefCell<Node>>>,
}
```

```
fn main() {
    let node1 = Rc::new(RefCell::new(Node { value: 1, next: None
}));
    let node2 = Rc::new(RefCell::new(Node { value: 2, next:
Some(Rc::clone(&node1)) }));

    node1.borrow_mut().next = Some(Rc::clone(&node2)); // Creates a
reference cycle
}
```

In this case, Rc creates a reference cycle, preventing memory from being freed. Rust
provides Weak<T> to break such cycles and prevent leaks.

Summary

Understanding stack vs. heap memory is crucial for writing efficient Rust programs. The
stack is fast, automatically managed, and suitable for small, fixed-size data. The heap
provides flexibility but requires explicit ownership management. By leveraging Rust's
ownership model and borrowing rules, developers can write memory-safe applications
without the need for garbage collection.

Smart Pointers and References

Memory management in Rust is built on the foundation of ownership, borrowing, and
lifetimes. However, for more complex scenarios, Rust provides **smart pointers**—specialized
data structures that offer enhanced memory management capabilities while ensuring safety
and efficiency. Smart pointers extend Rust's ownership system by automatically managing
heap allocations and reference counting. They enable dynamic memory management
without the need for a garbage collector.

What Are Smart Pointers?

A **smart pointer** is a wrapper around a pointer that provides additional functionality, such as
reference counting, interior mutability, or heap allocation management. Unlike regular
references (&T and &mut T), smart pointers own the data they point to and may include
additional logic for memory handling.

Rust's standard library includes several smart pointer types, each serving a different
purpose:

- Box<T> – Allocates data on the heap.
- Rc<T> – A reference-counted pointer for shared ownership.
- Arc<T> – An atomic reference-counted pointer for concurrent programs.
- RefCell<T> – Allows interior mutability by enforcing borrowing rules at runtime.

- `Weak<T>` – A non-owning reference to prevent reference cycles.

Understanding when and how to use smart pointers is crucial for writing efficient, safe Rust programs.

Box<T>: Storing Data on the Heap

The `Box<T>` smart pointer is the simplest way to allocate data on the heap. It is useful when:

- You want to store large data structures that exceed stack size limitations.
- You need a type with a known size at compile time but want dynamic dispatch (e.g., trait objects).
- You are working with recursive data structures.

Example: Using `Box<T>` for Heap Allocation

```
fn main() {
    let heap_number = Box::new(42); // Allocate an integer on the
heap
    println!("Heap-stored value: {}", heap_number);
} // heap_number goes out of scope and memory is freed
```

Here, `Box::new(42)` allocates an integer on the heap, while the `heap_number` variable (a pointer to this memory) is stored on the stack. When `heap_number` goes out of scope, Rust automatically deallocates the heap memory.

Example: Recursive Data Structures

A common use case for `Box<T>` is recursive data structures, such as linked lists:

```
enum List {
    Node(i32, Box<List>),
    Nil,
}

fn main() {
    let list = List::Node(1, Box::new(List::Node(2,
Box::new(List::Nil))));
}
```

Since Rust requires all types to have a known size at compile time, a recursive structure like `List` would be problematic if stored directly on the stack. Using `Box<T>`, we ensure that each node is allocated on the heap, making recursion possible.

Rc<T>: Reference Counting for Shared Ownership

In Rust's ownership model, a value can only have one owner at a time. However, sometimes multiple parts of a program need to share ownership of a value. This is where `Rc<T>` (Reference Counting) comes in.

`Rc<T>` is used in single-threaded programs where multiple references to the same heap-allocated data are required. It keeps track of the number of references to a value and only deallocates it when the reference count drops to zero.

Example: Shared Ownership with `Rc<T>`

```rust
use std::rc::Rc;

fn main() {
    let shared_value = Rc::new(100);

    let ref1 = Rc::clone(&shared_value);
    let ref2 = Rc::clone(&shared_value);

    println!("Reference Count: {}",
Rc::strong_count(&shared_value));
}
```

Here, `Rc::clone(&shared_value)` creates multiple references, and `Rc::strong_count` tracks how many active references exist. When all references go out of scope, Rust automatically frees the memory.

Key points about `Rc<T>`:

- It allows multiple ownership of heap-allocated data.
- It is only for single-threaded scenarios (use `Arc<T>` for multi-threading).
- Reference cycles can lead to memory leaks (use `Weak<T>` to prevent this).

Arc<T>: Thread-Safe Reference Counting

The `Arc<T>` (Atomic Reference Counted) smart pointer is similar to `Rc<T>`, but it is **thread-safe**. It uses atomic operations to maintain reference counts, making it safe for concurrent access across multiple threads.

Example: Using `Arc<T>` for Multi-Threading

```
use std::sync::Arc;
use std::thread;

fn main() {
    let shared_value = Arc::new(100);

    let handles: Vec<_> = (0..5).map(|_| {
        let shared_value = Arc::clone(&shared_value);
        thread::spawn(move || {
            println!("Value: {}", shared_value);
        })
    }).collect();

    for handle in handles {
        handle.join().unwrap();
    }
}
```

Here, `Arc::clone` ensures that multiple threads can safely reference the same value. Unlike `Rc<T>`, `Arc<T>` is designed for concurrent environments.

RefCell<T>: Interior Mutability

In Rust, borrowing rules enforce strict mutability constraints:

- Immutable references (`&T`) prevent mutation.
- Mutable references (`&mut T`) require exclusive access.

Sometimes, you may need to mutate a value while maintaining multiple references. This is where `RefCell<T>` comes in—it allows **interior mutability**, enforcing borrowing rules at runtime instead of compile time.

Example: Interior Mutability with `RefCell<T>`

```
use std::cell::RefCell;
```

```
fn main() {
    let value = RefCell::new(10);

    *value.borrow_mut() += 5;
    println!("Updated value: {}", value.borrow());
}
```

Here, `borrow_mut()` allows mutation within an immutable `RefCell<T>`, bypassing Rust's usual compile-time checks.

Caution: Since borrowing rules are enforced at runtime, improper usage (e.g., creating multiple mutable references) will result in a panic.

Weak<T>: Preventing Reference Cycles

`Rc<T>` can lead to memory leaks if reference cycles are created. To prevent this, Rust provides `Weak<T>`, which holds a **non-owning** reference to an `Rc<T>`-managed value.

Example: Breaking Cycles with `Weak<T>`

```
use std::rc::{Rc, Weak};
use std::cell::RefCell;

struct Node {
    value: i32,
    next: Option<Rc<RefCell<Node>>>,
    prev: Option<Weak<RefCell<Node>>>,
}

fn main() {
    let first = Rc::new(RefCell::new(Node { value: 1, next: None,
prev: None }));
    let second = Rc::new(RefCell::new(Node { value: 2, next: None,
prev: Some(Rc::downgrade(&first)) }));

    first.borrow_mut().next = Some(Rc::clone(&second));
}
```

By using `Weak<T>`, we prevent reference cycles that would otherwise lead to memory leaks.

Choosing the Right Smart Pointer

Smart Pointer	Use Case
`Box<T>`	Storing data on the heap
`Rc<T>`	Shared ownership in single-threaded applications
`Arc<T>`	Shared ownership in multi-threaded applications
`RefCell<T>`	Interior mutability with dynamic borrowing checks
`Weak<T>`	Preventing reference cycles in `Rc<T>`

Conclusion

Smart pointers are a powerful feature in Rust, providing efficient, safe memory management. `Box<T>` enables heap allocation, `Rc<T>` and `Arc<T>` facilitate shared ownership, `RefCell<T>` enables interior mutability, and `Weak<T>` prevents memory leaks. By understanding these tools, developers can write robust and efficient Rust programs while maintaining strict memory safety guarantees.

Rust's Borrow Checker in Action

Rust's ownership model is enforced by the **borrow checker**, a component of the compiler that ensures safe memory access without data races or invalid memory access. The borrow checker plays a crucial role in preventing issues like use-after-free, double free, and dangling references by enforcing strict ownership and borrowing rules at compile time.

Understanding how the borrow checker works and how to resolve borrowing-related errors is essential for writing efficient and safe Rust programs.

Ownership Recap

Rust's memory management revolves around **ownership**, where each value has a single owner. When an owner goes out of scope, Rust automatically deallocates the associated memory. Ownership can be **moved** or **borrowed**.

```
fn main() {
    let s1 = String::from("hello");
    let s2 = s1; // Ownership moves to s2

    // println!("{}", s1); // ERROR: s1 is no longer valid
}
```

Here, s1 is moved to s2, so s1 is no longer accessible. This prevents double-free errors but requires careful handling of ownership transfers.

Borrowing in Rust

To allow multiple references to a value without transferring ownership, Rust provides **borrowing**. Borrowing comes in two forms:

1. **Immutable borrowing** (&T) – Multiple reads are allowed, but no modifications.

2. **Mutable borrowing** (&mut T) – Only one mutable reference is allowed at a time.

Example: Immutable Borrowing

```
fn print_length(s: &String) {
    println!("Length: {}", s.len());
}

fn main() {
    let s = String::from("hello");
    print_length(&s); // Borrowing s, ownership remains with main
    println!("{}", s); // Still valid
}
```

Since print_length takes a reference (&String), ownership remains with main, and s can still be used after the function call.

Example: Mutable Borrowing

```
fn add_exclamation(s: &mut String) {
    s.push_str("!");
}
```

```
fn main() {
    let mut s = String::from("hello");
    add_exclamation(&mut s); // Mutably borrowing s
    println!("{}", s);
}
```

Here, &mut s is passed to add_exclamation, allowing mutation while enforcing that only one mutable reference exists at a time.

Borrowing Rules

Rust's borrow checker enforces the following rules:

- You can have **multiple immutable references** (&T) OR **one mutable reference** (&mut T), but not both.

- References **must always be valid** (i.e., no use-after-free).

- Mutable references cannot exist alongside immutable ones.

Example: Conflicting Borrow

```
fn main() {
    let mut s = String::from("hello");

    let r1 = &s;
    let r2 = &s;
    let r3 = &mut s; // ERROR: Cannot have a mutable reference while
r1 and r2 exist

    println!("{}, {}", r1, r2);
}
```

The borrow checker prevents simultaneous mutable and immutable references to ensure safe concurrent access.

Lifetimes and the Borrow Checker

Lifetimes define how long references are valid. The borrow checker ensures references **never outlive the data they point to**, preventing dangling references.

Example: Dangling Reference (Compile-Time Error)

```
fn dangle() -> &String {
    let s = String::from("hello");
    &s // ERROR: s is deallocated at function exit
}
```

The function `dangle` tries to return a reference to a variable that is deallocated when the function exits, causing an invalid reference.

To fix this, return an owned value:

```
fn no_dangle() -> String {
    String::from("hello") // Ownership is moved, no reference issue
}
```

The Role of Lifetimes in Borrowing

Lifetimes explicitly define how long borrowed references remain valid. Rust infers lifetimes in most cases, but sometimes they need to be specified explicitly.

Example: Explicit Lifetime Annotations

```
fn longest<'a>(s1: &'a str, s2: &'a str) -> &'a str {
    if s1.len() > s2.len() {
        s1
    } else {
        s2
    }
}
```

Here, `'a` ensures that the returned reference is valid as long as both `s1` and `s2` are.

Interior Mutability and the Borrow Checker

Rust enforces borrowing rules at compile time, but some cases require modifying data through an immutable reference. **Interior mutability** allows this by enforcing borrowing rules at runtime instead.

Example: Interior Mutability with `RefCell<T>`

```
use std::cell::RefCell;

fn main() {
    let value = RefCell::new(42);

    *value.borrow_mut() += 1;
    println!("{}", value.borrow());
}
```

`RefCell<T>` allows mutable borrowing inside an immutable value, but it enforces borrow rules at runtime rather than compile time.

Borrow Checker Errors and Fixes

The borrow checker often catches errors that lead to memory corruption in other languages. Here are some common errors and how to fix them.

1. Mutable and Immutable Borrowing Conflict

Error Code:

```
fn main() {
    let mut data = String::from("Rust");

    let r1 = &data;
    let r2 = &data;
    let r3 = &mut data; // ERROR: Cannot borrow mutably when
immutable borrows exist

    println!("{}, {}", r1, r2);
}
```

Fix: Move r3 to a new scope so the immutable borrows are no longer active.

```
fn main() {
    let mut data = String::from("Rust");

    {
        let r1 = &data;
        let r2 = &data;
        println!("{}, {}", r1, r2);
    } // r1 and r2 go out of scope

    let r3 = &mut data; // Now valid
    println!("{}", r3);
}
```

---

2. Returning a Reference to a Local Variable

Error Code:

```
fn get_ref() -> &String {
    let s = String::from("hello");
    &s // ERROR: `s` is dropped when function exits
}
```

Fix: Return an owned value instead.

```
fn get_owned() -> String {
    String::from("hello") // No reference issue
}
```

---

3. Borrowing Data that May Be Mutated

Error Code:

```
use std::cell::RefCell;

fn main() {
    let data = RefCell::new(5);
```

```
    let ref1 = data.borrow();
    let ref2 = data.borrow_mut(); // ERROR: Cannot borrow mutably
while immutable borrow exists
}
```

Fix: Ensure all immutable borrows are dropped before creating a mutable borrow.

```
fn main() {
    let data = RefCell::new(5);

    {
        let ref1 = data.borrow();
        println!("{}", ref1);
    } // ref1 goes out of scope

    let ref2 = data.borrow_mut();
    *ref2 += 1;
}
```

Summary

The borrow checker is a core part of Rust's memory safety guarantees. By enforcing strict ownership and borrowing rules, it prevents memory corruption, dangling references, and data races. Understanding how to work with the borrow checker—using borrowing rules, lifetimes, and interior mutability—enables developers to write safe and efficient Rust code without a garbage collector.

By leveraging borrowing correctly, developers can take full advantage of Rust's unique approach to memory management while avoiding common pitfalls encountered in other low-level languages.

Handling Memory Leaks and Unsafe Rust

Rust is celebrated for its memory safety, achieved without a garbage collector, thanks to its ownership and borrowing model. However, despite these robust safeguards, memory leaks can still occur. Rust prevents many common memory errors like use-after-free, double free, or data races, but **logical leaks**—where memory is still technically reachable but never freed—are still possible. This section explores how memory leaks can arise in safe Rust, how to prevent them, and how to use **unsafe Rust** responsibly when performance or low-level access is required.

Memory Leaks in Safe Rust

In Rust, memory leaks occur when memory is no longer needed but not deallocated because references to it still exist. The most common cause is **reference cycles**, typically involving Rc<T> (reference-counted smart pointers).

Example: Reference Cycle with Rc and RefCell

```rust
use std::rc::Rc;

use std::cell::RefCell;


#[derive(Debug)]

struct Node {

    value: i32,

    next: Option<Rc<RefCell<Node>>>,

}


fn main() {

    let first = Rc::new(RefCell::new(Node { value: 1, next: None
}));

    let second = Rc::new(RefCell::new(Node { value: 2, next:
Some(Rc::clone(&first)) }));


    // Create a cycle

    first.borrow_mut().next = Some(Rc::clone(&second));


    // At this point, both nodes reference each other and will never
be dropped.

}
```

The example above creates a **reference cycle** between `first` and `second`, making both nodes leak memory because their reference counts never reach zero.

Detecting Memory Leaks

Rust doesn't provide built-in leak detection, but you can use external tools like:

- **Valgrind**: General-purpose memory debugging.

- **Heaptrack**: Tracks heap memory allocations.

- `cargo-valgrind`: Integration with Valgrind.

- `cargo-geiger`: Helps find unsafe code which may contribute to leaks.

You can also use the `Rc::strong_count` and `Rc::weak_count` functions to monitor reference counts and detect potential leaks in logic.

Breaking Cycles with Weak References

To prevent reference cycles, use `Weak<T>`, which does not increment the strong reference count. This allows one direction of a relationship to not own the other.

Example: Fixing Reference Cycle with Weak

```rust
use std::rc::{Rc, Weak};

use std::cell::RefCell;


#[derive(Debug)]

struct Node {

    value: i32,

    parent: RefCell<Weak<Node>>,

    children: RefCell<Vec<Rc<Node>>>,

}
```

```
fn main() {

    let leaf = Rc::new(Node {

        value: 3,

        parent: RefCell::new(Weak::new()),

        children: RefCell::new(vec![]),

    });


    let branch = Rc::new(Node {

        value: 5,

        parent: RefCell::new(Weak::new()),

        children: RefCell::new(vec![Rc::clone(&leaf)]),

    });


    *leaf.parent.borrow_mut() = Rc::downgrade(&branch);

}
```

In this example, the child node (leaf) holds a **weak reference** to its parent (branch), preventing a reference cycle.

Leaking Memory Intentionally

In rare cases, it might be desirable to **intentionally leak memory**, especially when interfacing with FFI (foreign function interface) or creating memory that must live for the duration of a program.

Rust provides a way to leak memory explicitly:

```
fn main() {

    let leaked = Box::leak(Box::new(100));

    println!("Leaked value: {}", leaked);

}
```

`Box::leak` converts a `Box<T>` into a `'static` reference by **intentionally not deallocating** it. The value will never be cleaned up unless manually managed via raw pointers or external mechanisms.

This is useful in some static initialization scenarios, but should be used sparingly and with clear intent.

Introduction to Unsafe Rust

Rust provides the `unsafe` keyword to allow operations that the compiler can't guarantee to be safe. Unsafe Rust lets you:

- Dereference raw pointers.

- Call unsafe functions (including FFI).

- Access mutable static variables.

- Implement unsafe traits.

- Perform unchecked memory operations.

Using `unsafe` is not inherently dangerous—but it's your responsibility to uphold Rust's safety guarantees manually.

```
fn main() {

    let x: i32 = 5;

    let r: *const i32 = &x;


    unsafe {
```

```
    println!("Value through raw pointer: {}", *r);

}

}
```

Here, the raw pointer *r bypasses the borrow checker, and we use an unsafe block to dereference it. While this works, dereferencing raw pointers without validation can lead to undefined behavior.

When to Use Unsafe

Unsafe Rust is essential in scenarios such as:

- Interfacing with C libraries (FFI).

- Building low-level data structures (e.g., arena allocators, memory pools).

- Performance-critical code that avoids bounds checks.

- Implementing abstractions that safe Rust can't express.

It is **not** meant for bypassing borrow checker errors due to poor program structure. The philosophy should be: use safe Rust *whenever possible*, and **unsafe only when necessary**, encapsulated and well-documented.

Encapsulating Unsafe Code

Best practice dictates that unsafe code should be **contained and hidden** behind safe abstractions. The unsafe code is tested and validated internally, and safe APIs are exposed to users.

Example: Safe Abstraction over Unsafe Code

```
struct MyBuffer {

    ptr: *mut u8,

    length: usize,
```

```rust
}


impl MyBuffer {

    fn new(size: usize) -> Self {

        let ptr = unsafe { libc::malloc(size) as *mut u8 };

        Self { ptr, length: size }

    }


    fn write(&mut self, offset: usize, byte: u8) {

        if offset < self.length {

            unsafe {

                *self.ptr.add(offset) = byte;

            }

        }

    }

}


impl Drop for MyBuffer {

    fn drop(&mut self) {

        unsafe {

            libc::free(self.ptr as *mut _);

        }

    }

}
```

Here, the unsafe logic is wrapped in `MyBuffer`. Users interact with safe methods like `write`, while the implementation takes care of low-level operations.

Tools for Auditing Unsafe Code

To manage unsafe code usage responsibly:

- Use `cargo-geiger` to scan for unsafe usage.

- Use linters and static analysis tools to validate invariants.

- Write thorough unit and integration tests around unsafe blocks.

- Document preconditions and invariants.

Alternatives to Unsafe

Before reaching for `unsafe`, consider:

- `RefCell<T>` for interior mutability.

- `Box<T>` or `Vec<T>` for manual memory management.

- Lifetimes and explicit borrowing for aliasing rules.

- Higher-level abstractions from crates like `crossbeam`, `rayon`, or `mio`.

Often, a refactor or deeper understanding of lifetimes and borrowing reveals a safe solution.

Summary

While Rust provides strong guarantees against memory errors, it is still possible to leak memory through reference cycles or intentional actions. By using tools like `Weak<T>` and following best practices, these can be mitigated. Additionally, `unsafe` Rust opens the door to low-level programming but must be used with caution, proper abstraction, and documentation.

Understanding how and when memory leaks occur, and how to harness the power of `unsafe`, gives developers the tools needed to build high-performance, low-level, yet still memory-safe systems in Rust.

Chapter 4: Working with Collections and Iterators

Vectors, Strings, and HashMaps

In any programming language, working with collections of data is a common and necessary task. Rust provides a powerful and safe set of standard library collections that enable developers to efficiently store, retrieve, and manipulate data. In this section, we'll delve into three of the most widely used collection types in Rust: `Vec`, `String`, and `HashMap`.

Vectors (`Vec<T>`)

Vectors are resizable arrays. Unlike arrays in Rust that have a fixed size known at compile time, vectors are stored on the heap and can grow or shrink at runtime.

Creating a Vector

There are several ways to create vectors in Rust:

```rust
fn main() {

    let mut numbers: Vec<i32> = Vec::new();

    numbers.push(1);

    numbers.push(2);

    numbers.push(3);


    println!("{:?}", numbers);

}
```

You can also use the `vec!` macro:

```rust
fn main() {
```

```rust
    let numbers = vec![1, 2, 3, 4, 5];

    println!("{:?}", numbers);

}
```

Accessing Elements

Elements in a vector can be accessed using indexing or the get method:

```rust
let numbers = vec![10, 20, 30, 40, 50];

let third = numbers[2];

let maybe_fourth = numbers.get(3);


println!("Third element: {}", third);

match maybe_fourth {

    Some(value) => println!("Fourth element: {}", value),

    None => println!("No fourth element."),

}
```

Using get is safer as it returns an Option, protecting against out-of-bounds access.

Iterating Over Vectors

```rust
let numbers = vec![1, 2, 3];

for num in &numbers {

    println!("{}", num);

}
```

You can also mutate values during iteration:

```
let mut numbers = vec![1, 2, 3];

for num in &mut numbers {

    *num += 10;

}

println!("{:?}", numbers);
```

Removing Elements

Use pop to remove the last element:

```
let mut numbers = vec![1, 2, 3];

numbers.pop();

println!("{:?}", numbers);
```

To remove elements at a specific index:

```
let mut numbers = vec![10, 20, 30, 40];

numbers.remove(1); // removes the second element (20)

println!("{:?}", numbers);
```

Strings

In Rust, strings come in two main forms: String and &str. The String type is a heap-allocated, growable string. &str is an immutable string slice.

Creating Strings

```rust
let mut greeting = String::from("Hello");

greeting.push_str(", world!");

println!("{}", greeting);
```

You can also concatenate strings:

```rust
let hello = String::from("Hello, ");

let world = "world!";

let combined = hello + world; // `hello` is moved here

println!("{}", combined);
```

For multiple concatenations, use `format!`:

```rust
let s1 = String::from("tic");

let s2 = String::from("tac");

let s3 = String::from("toe");


let game = format!("{}-{}-{}", s1, s2, s3);

println!("{}", game);
```

Accessing String Data

Rust strings are UTF-8 encoded, so direct indexing into them is not allowed. Instead, use slicing:

```rust
let hello = "Здравствуйте";

let s = &hello[0..4]; // first two characters in UTF-8

println!("{}", s);
```

To iterate over characters or bytes:

```rust
for c in "hello".chars() {

    println!("{}", c);

}


for b in "hello".bytes() {

    println!("{}", b);

}
```

HashMaps

HashMaps store key-value pairs and are useful for situations where you want to look up data by a specific key.

Creating and Using a HashMap

```rust
use std::collections::HashMap;


fn main() {

    let mut scores = HashMap::new();

    scores.insert(String::from("Blue"), 10);
```

```rust
    scores.insert(String::from("Red"), 50);


    println!("{:?}", scores);
}
```

You can retrieve values using `get`:

```rust
let team_name = String::from("Blue");
if let Some(score) = scores.get(&team_name) {
    println!("Score: {}", score);
}
```

Iterating Over a HashMap

```rust
for (key, value) in &scores {
    println!("{}: {}", key, value);
}
```

Updating Values

To overwrite an existing value:

```rust
scores.insert(String::from("Blue"), 25);
```

To insert only if the key has no value yet:

```
scores.entry(String::from("Green")).or_insert(30);
```

To update based on the old value:

```
let text = "hello world wonderful world";

let mut map = HashMap::new();

for word in text.split_whitespace() {
    let count = map.entry(word).or_insert(0);
    *count += 1;
}

println!("{:?}", map);
```

Choosing the Right Collection

Rust's collections are designed for performance and safety. Here's a quick guide for when to use each:

- Use `Vec<T>` when you need an ordered collection with fast indexing and iteration.

- Use `String` for dynamic textual data you want to mutate.

- Use `HashMap<K, V>` when you need fast key-based lookup.

Each of these collections complements Rust's strict safety and ownership rules, ensuring memory safety without needing a garbage collector.

Common Pitfalls and Best Practices

1. **Avoid Indexing Strings Directly**: Due to UTF-8 encoding, slicing improperly may panic at runtime.

2. **Use `get` Instead of Indexing in Vectors**: Indexing directly may panic if out of bounds.

3. **Clone When Necessary**: When working with owned data in `HashMap`, sometimes cloning is unavoidable.

4. **Use Entry API**: The `entry` API in `HashMap` helps avoid unnecessary lookups and enables compound operations.

Performance Considerations

- `Vec` offers constant time `push` operations and fast indexing.

- `String` has amortized $O(1)$ for `push_str`.

- `HashMap` uses a randomized hash algorithm to prevent collision attacks, but insertion and lookup are $O(1)$ on average.

Always profile and benchmark for performance-critical code (covered in Chapter 9).

Conclusion

Collections form the foundation of real-world data manipulation in Rust. With `Vec`, `String`, and `HashMap`, Rust provides flexible and efficient tools that uphold its core principles of memory safety and zero-cost abstractions. Mastery of these types is essential for building robust and idiomatic Rust programs.

Iterators and Closures

Rust's iterators and closures are core features that provide powerful, expressive, and memory-safe ways to manipulate collections and other sequences of data. Iterators in Rust are lazy, composable, and zero-cost abstractions, while closures let you define functions inline, capturing the surrounding environment as needed. Together, they unlock a functional programming style that blends seamlessly with Rust's ownership and type system.

Understanding Iterators

An *iterator* is any type that implements the `Iterator` trait. This trait has a single required method:

```
trait Iterator {

    type Item;


    fn next(&mut self) -> Option<Self::Item>;

}
```

Calling `next()` on an iterator returns `Some(item)` as long as there are elements, and `None` when the iterator is finished.

Basic Iterator Usage

```
fn main() {

    let v = vec![1, 2, 3];

    let mut iter = v.iter();


    assert_eq!(iter.next(), Some(&1));

    assert_eq!(iter.next(), Some(&2));

    assert_eq!(iter.next(), Some(&3));

    assert_eq!(iter.next(), None);

}
```

Here, `v.iter()` creates an iterator that yields references to the elements in the vector.

Consuming vs. Adapting Iterators

Rust provides two primary ways to interact with iterators:

- **Consumer methods**, which use the iterator and consume it.

- **Adapter methods**, which return a new iterator with modified behavior.

Consuming Adaptors

Common consuming adaptors include:

- `collect()`: gathers items into a collection.

- `sum()`: sums numeric items.

- `count()`: counts elements.

- `last()`: returns the last item.

- `nth(n)`: returns the nth element.

```
let v = vec![1, 2, 3, 4, 5];

let sum: i32 = v.iter().sum();

println!("Sum is {}", sum);
```

Iterator Adapters

Adapter methods return new iterators and are usually chained together before being consumed:

- `map()`

- `filter()`

- `enumerate()`

- `take()`, `skip()`

- `chain()`

- `zip()`

```
let numbers = vec![1, 2, 3, 4, 5];

let squared: Vec<_> = numbers.iter().map(|x| x * x).collect();

println!("{:?}", squared);
```

This example uses `map` to square each number and then collects the results into a new `Vec`.

Closures

Closures are anonymous functions that can capture variables from their surrounding scope. They are declared with the `|args| expr` syntax.

```
let add = |a, b| a + b;

println!("{}", add(3, 4));
```

Capturing the Environment

Closures automatically capture variables from their environment by reference, by mutable reference, or by value, depending on how the closure is used:

```
let name = String::from("Rust");

let say_hello = || println!("Hello, {}!", name);

say_hello();
```

To mutate captured variables:

```
let mut count = 0;
let mut add_one = || count += 1;

add_one();
add_one();

println!("Count is: {}", count);
```

To move a variable into the closure:

```
let data = vec![1, 2, 3];
let consume = move || {
    println!("{:?}", data);
};
// data is moved into the closure
consume();
```

Combining Iterators and Closures

The real power of closures comes when used with iterators. Consider the following:

```
let numbers = vec![1, 2, 3, 4, 5];
```

```
let evens: Vec<_> = numbers.iter().filter(|&x| x % 2 ==
0).collect();
```

```
println!("{:?}", evens); // [2, 4]
```

Here, `filter` takes a closure that returns `true` for even numbers. The closure captures `x` by reference from the iterator.

Another example using `map` and `filter`:

```
let v = vec![1, 2, 3, 4, 5, 6];

let doubled_evens: Vec<_> = v.iter()

    .filter(|&x| x % 2 == 0)

    .map(|x| x * 2)

    .collect();
```

```
println!("{:?}", doubled_evens); // [4, 8, 12]
```

Chaining Iterator Adapters

Rust encourages composition through method chaining. The following code demonstrates a multi-step transformation:

```
let names = vec!["Alice", "Bob", "Carol", "Dave"];

let abbreviated: Vec<_> = names.iter()

    .filter(|name| name.len() <= 4)

    .map(|name| name.to_uppercase())
```

```
        .collect();
```

```
println!("{:?}", abbreviated); // ["BOB", "DAVE"]
```

Each step is performed lazily, and computation only occurs during the final `collect()` call.

Consuming Infinite Iterators

Iterators can be infinite. Use `take(n)` to safely consume a portion:

```
let squares: Vec<_> = (1..).map(|x| x * x).take(5).collect();
println!("{:?}", squares); // [1, 4, 9, 16, 25]
```

Enumerate, Zip, and Chain

- `enumerate()` adds a counter:

```
for (i, val) in ["a", "b", "c"].iter().enumerate() {
    println!("{}: {}", i, val);
}
```

- `zip()` combines two iterators:

```
let letters = ['a', 'b', 'c'];
let numbers = [1, 2, 3];
```

```
for pair in letters.iter().zip(numbers.iter()) {

    println!("{:?}", pair);

}
```

- chain() joins two iterators:

```
let a = vec![1, 2, 3];

let b = vec![4, 5];


let combined: Vec<_> = a.iter().chain(b.iter()).collect();

println!("{:?}", combined); // [1, 2, 3, 4, 5]
```

Custom Iterators

You can implement the Iterator trait for your own types:

```
struct Counter {

    count: u32,

}


impl Counter {

    fn new() -> Counter {

        Counter { count: 0 }
```

```
    }

}


impl Iterator for Counter {

    type Item = u32;


    fn next(&mut self) -> Option<Self::Item> {

        self.count += 1;

        if self.count <= 5 {

            Some(self.count)

        } else {

            None

        }

    }

}


let counter = Counter::new();

for val in counter {

    println!("{}", val);

}
```

This prints 1 through 5. Custom iterators enable complex patterns and structures to be traversed idiomatically.

Practical Use Cases

Parsing and transforming log data:

```
let logs = vec!["INFO start", "ERROR fail", "INFO done"];
let errors: Vec<_> = logs.iter()
    .filter(|entry| entry.starts_with("ERROR"))
    .map(|e| e.to_string())
    .collect();
```

Summing filtered numbers:

```
let nums = vec![10, 15, 20, 25, 30];
let sum: i32 = nums.into_iter()
    .filter(|n| n % 10 == 0)
    .sum();

println!("{}", sum); // 60
```

Building custom reports:

```
let sales = vec![100, 200, 150, 50, 400];
let high_sales: Vec<_> = sales.iter()
    .enumerate()
    .filter(|(_, &value)| value > 150)
    .map(|(index, &value)| format!("Day {}: ${}", index + 1, value))
    .collect();
```

```
for line in high_sales {

    println!("{}", line);

}
```

Summary

Rust's iterator and closure system combines performance and elegance. Key points:

- Iterators provide lazy, composable operations on sequences.

- Closures are anonymous functions that capture their environment.

- Method chaining with iterators enables concise and readable logic.

- `map`, `filter`, and `collect` are cornerstones of functional-style programming in Rust.

- You can extend functionality by implementing the `Iterator` trait.

By mastering iterators and closures, you gain access to one of the most expressive and efficient parts of the Rust language—capable of powering everything from simple loops to complex data processing pipelines.

Using Traits and Generics for Flexible Code

Traits and generics form the foundation of polymorphism in Rust. Together, they provide a way to write abstract, reusable, and type-safe code without sacrificing performance. Unlike traditional object-oriented languages that often rely on dynamic dispatch and inheritance hierarchies, Rust achieves code reuse and abstraction through static dispatch and trait-based programming. This section explores how to define and use traits, implement generics, and combine them to create flexible and robust software architectures.

Traits: Interfaces in Rust

A *trait* in Rust defines shared behavior. It is similar to an interface in other languages like Java or C#. Traits allow you to define method signatures that multiple types can implement.

Defining and Implementing Traits

Here is a simple trait definition and implementation:

```rust
trait Speak {

    fn speak(&self) -> String;

}


struct Dog;

struct Cat;


impl Speak for Dog {

    fn speak(&self) -> String {

        String::from("Woof!")

    }

}


impl Speak for Cat {

    fn speak(&self) -> String {

        String::from("Meow!")

    }

}


fn main() {

    let dog = Dog;

    let cat = Cat;
```

```
    println!("{}", dog.speak());

    println!("{}", cat.speak());

}
```

Traits allow you to define functionality in a generic and extensible way.

Trait Bounds and Generics

To use traits with generics, you apply *trait bounds*. This constrains a generic type to types that implement a specific trait.

```
fn make_sound<T: Speak>(animal: T) {

    println!("{}", animal.speak());

}
```

Or with the where clause for readability:

```
fn make_sound<T>(animal: T)

where

    T: Speak,

{

    println!("{}", animal.speak());

}
```

Trait bounds are central to generic programming in Rust. They ensure that generic types support the required operations.

Generic Data Structures

Generics allow data structures to work with any type, improving code reuse and type safety.

```
struct Pair<T> {

    first: T,

    second: T,

}


impl<T> Pair<T> {

    fn new(first: T, second: T) -> Self {

        Pair { first, second }

    }

}
```

You can also conditionally implement methods based on trait bounds:

```
impl<T: std::fmt::Display> Pair<T> {

    fn display(&self) {

        println!("({}, {})", self.first, self.second);

    }

}
```

This adds the `display` method only when T implements `Display`.

Default Method Implementations in Traits

You can provide default implementations for trait methods:

```rust
trait Greet {
    fn greet(&self) {
        println!("Hello!");
    }
}

struct Person;

impl Greet for Person {} // Uses the default greet

fn main() {
    let p = Person;
    p.greet();
}
```

This is useful for providing behavior that can be overridden but doesn't have to be.

Traits as Parameters and Return Types

Rust allows you to accept or return types implementing a trait using two approaches:

Trait Bounds with Generics

```rust
fn print_speak<T: Speak>(item: T) {
```

```
    println!("{}", item.speak());

}
```

Trait Objects (Dynamic Dispatch)

```
fn print_speak_dyn(item: &dyn Speak) {

    println!("{}", item.speak());

}
```

With trait objects, you gain runtime polymorphism at the cost of some performance. This is useful when the exact type is not known at compile time.

Returning Trait Objects

```
fn get_animal(name: &str) -> Box<dyn Speak> {

    if name == "dog" {

        Box::new(Dog)

    } else {

        Box::new(Cat)

    }

}
```

Note the use of `Box<dyn Trait>` for heap allocation and dynamic dispatch.

Implementing Multiple Traits

A single type can implement multiple traits:

```rust
trait Walk {

    fn walk(&self);

}


trait Run {

    fn run(&self);

}


struct Human;


impl Walk for Human {

    fn walk(&self) {

        println!("Walking...");

    }

}


impl Run for Human {

    fn run(&self) {

        println!("Running!");

    }

}
```

Functions can then use multiple bounds:

```rust
fn move_fast<T: Walk + Run>(person: T) {
```

```
    person.walk();

    person.run();

}
```

Generic Functions

Rust functions can be generic over any type:

```
fn identity<T>(x: T) -> T {

    x

}
```

```
fn main() {

    let a = identity(10);

    let b = identity("hello");


    println!("a: {}, b: {}", a, b);

}
```

The compiler infers the type of T automatically.

Generic Enums and Structs

You can define enums and structs with generic types:

```
enum Option<T> {
```

```
    Some(T),

    None,

}


struct Container<T, U> {

    x: T,

    y: U,

}
```

This enables highly reusable, type-safe abstractions.

Associated Types

Associated types are an alternative to generics when defining traits:

```
trait Iterator {

    type Item;


    fn next(&mut self) -> Option<Self::Item>;

}
```

Here, Item is an associated type, defined once per implementation, rather than passing it in as a generic parameter everywhere the trait is used.

Blanket Implementations

Rust allows you to implement a trait for any type that satisfies certain conditions:

```rust
trait Print {

    fn print(&self);

}


impl<T: std::fmt::Display> Print for T {

    fn print(&self) {

        println!("{}", self);

    }

}


fn main() {

    let x = 42;

    x.print(); // Works because i32 implements Display

}
```

This pattern is very common in the standard library and powerful for extending functionality.

Limitations and Workarounds

1. **Traits Cannot Have Fields**: Traits define behavior, not state. You cannot define fields in a trait.

2. **Trait Inheritance Is Explicit**: Traits can extend other traits:

```rust
trait Animal {

    fn name(&self) -> String;
```

```
}


trait Pet: Animal {

    fn cuddle(&self);

}
```

3. **No Overloading Based on Return Type**: Rust does not allow function overloading or disambiguation based on return types.

4. **Monomorphization Bloat**: Extensive use of generics can lead to binary size increases. Use trait objects when appropriate to reduce duplication.

Real-World Example: Logger Trait

```
trait Logger {

    fn log(&self, message: &str);

}


struct ConsoleLogger;


impl Logger for ConsoleLogger {

    fn log(&self, message: &str) {

        println!("[console] {}", message);

    }

}
```

```
struct FileLogger;


impl Logger for FileLogger {

    fn log(&self, message: &str) {

        // Normally you'd write to a file

        println!("[file] {}", message);

    }

}


fn write_log<T: Logger>(logger: &T, msg: &str) {

    logger.log(msg);

}
```

This decouples logging logic from the output medium.

Advanced Pattern: Trait Objects and Composition

Combining different objects implementing the same trait:

```
let loggers: Vec<Box<dyn Logger>> = vec![

    Box::new(ConsoleLogger),

    Box::new(FileLogger),

];


for logger in loggers {

    logger.log("An event occurred");
```

```
}
```

This pattern is useful in plugin architectures or systems with pluggable behavior.

Summary

Traits and generics are foundational in Rust for writing abstract, flexible, and type-safe code. Key takeaways include:

- Traits define shared behavior and can have default implementations.

- Generics allow you to write reusable code without sacrificing safety or performance.

- Trait bounds restrict generic types to those that implement specific traits.

- Trait objects enable dynamic polymorphism at runtime.

- Associated types simplify trait usage in complex scenarios.

- Blanket implementations allow powerful extensions for entire groups of types.

Mastering traits and generics is essential to building idiomatic, maintainable, and performant Rust programs. They unlock expressive design patterns and allow your code to scale with complexity while maintaining safety and clarity.

Error Handling: Result and Option Types

Error handling is an essential part of writing robust and resilient software. In Rust, error handling is not based on exceptions or panic-recovery mechanisms found in many other languages. Instead, Rust promotes explicit and predictable handling of both recoverable and unrecoverable errors through two powerful enum types: `Option<T>` and `Result<T, E>`.

These enums make it easy to express error conditions without runtime surprises, enforcing compile-time checks that ensure errors are considered and handled appropriately. This section dives deep into how `Option` and `Result` work, how to use them effectively, and the idiomatic patterns for dealing with errors in real-world applications.

The `Option` Type

The `Option<T>` enum is used when a value may or may not be present. It is defined as:

```
enum Option<T> {

    Some(T),

    None,

}
```

You can think of `Option` as a safer alternative to null. In Rust, `None` is explicitly handled, avoiding null reference errors at runtime.

Using `Option` in Practice

```
fn find_even_number(numbers: &[i32]) -> Option<i32> {

    for &num in numbers {

        if num % 2 == 0 {

            return Some(num);

        }

    }

    None

}
```

```
fn main() {

    let values = vec![1, 3, 5, 8, 9];

    match find_even_number(&values) {

        Some(even) => println!("Found even number: {}", even),

        None => println!("No even number found."),
```

```
        }

}
```

Common Methods on `Option`

Rust provides many helpful methods for working with `Option`:

- `is_some()`, `is_none()`
- `unwrap()`, `expect()`
- `map()`, `and_then()`
- `unwrap_or()`, `unwrap_or_else()`
- `filter()`

```
let name: Option<String> = Some("Rust".to_string());


let length = name.map(|n| n.len()).unwrap_or(0);

println!("Name length: {}", length);
```

The method `map()` applies a function if the value is Some, and passes through None otherwise.

The `Result` Type

The `Result<T, E>` enum is used for operations that can succeed (`Ok`) or fail (`Err`). It is defined as:

```
enum Result<T, E> {

    Ok(T),
```

```
        Err(E),

}
```

This is the standard way to handle recoverable errors in Rust.

Basic Example

```
fn divide(x: i32, y: i32) -> Result<i32, String> {

    if y == 0 {

        Err(String::from("Cannot divide by zero"))

    } else {

        Ok(x / y)

    }

}


fn main() {

    match divide(10, 2) {

        Ok(result) => println!("Result: {}", result),

        Err(e) => println!("Error: {}", e),

    }

}
```

Using `Result` requires you to handle both success and failure cases.

Unwrapping with Caution

You can use `unwrap()` or `expect()` to get the value from `Option` or `Result`, but doing so will panic if the variant is `None` or `Err`.

```rust
let result: Result<i32, &str> = Ok(42);

println!("Value: {}", result.unwrap()); // Works
```

```rust
let result: Result<i32, &str> = Err("Oops");

// result.unwrap(); // Panics
```

`expect()` lets you customize the panic message:

```rust
result.expect("Expected a successful result, got an error instead");
```

These are useful in prototyping or when failure is impossible by logic, but generally discouraged in production.

Error Propagation with ?

The `?` operator is used to propagate errors up the call stack:

```rust
fn read_number() -> Result<i32, std::num::ParseIntError> {

    let input = "42";

    let num = input.parse::<i32>()?;

    Ok(num)

}
```

This is shorthand for:

```
let num = match input.parse::<i32>() {

    Ok(n) => n,

    Err(e) => return Err(e),

};
```

You can only use ? in functions that return Result or Option.

Chaining Methods

The composability of Option and Result makes chaining easy:

```
let input = Some("42");

let result = input

    .map(|s| s.parse::<i32>())

    .transpose();


match result {

    Ok(Some(n)) => println!("Parsed: {}", n),

    Ok(None) => println!("No value to parse."),

    Err(e) => println!("Parse error: {}", e),

}
```

This example uses transpose() to convert Option<Result<T, E>> to Result<Option<T>, E>, allowing elegant handling of optional parsing.

Working with `and_then` and `map`

These methods allow chaining computations that might fail:

```rust
fn square_root(x: f64) -> Option<f64> {
    if x >= 0.0 {
        Some(x.sqrt())
    } else {
        None
    }
}


fn main() {
    let result = Some(25.0)
        .and_then(square_root)
        .and_then(square_root);

    println!("{:?}", result); // Some(2.236...)
}
```

`and_then()` is especially useful when the next operation also returns an `Option` or `Result`.

Defining Your Own Error Types

For complex systems, define your own error types:

```
#[derive(Debug)]

enum AppError {

    Io(std::io::Error),

    Parse(std::num::ParseIntError),

}


fn read_and_parse() -> Result<i32, AppError> {

    let data =
std::fs::read_to_string("numbers.txt").map_err(AppError::Io)?;

    let number =
data.trim().parse::<i32>().map_err(AppError::Parse)?;

    Ok(number)

}
```

This gives you type-safe, granular error handling.

Using `thiserror` and `anyhow`

For ergonomic error handling, popular crates include:

- `thiserror`: for creating custom error types with minimal boilerplate.

- `anyhow`: for applications where you don't care about exact error types.

```
use thiserror::Error;


#[derive(Error, Debug)]

enum MyError {
```

```
    #[error("IO error")]

    Io(#[from] std::io::Error),


    #[error("Parse error")]

    Parse(#[from] std::num::ParseIntError),

}
```

With anyhow:

```
use anyhow::{Result, Context};


fn run() -> Result<()> {

    let data = std::fs::read_to_string("config.toml")

        .context("Failed to read config file")?;


    let value: i32 = data.trim().parse()

        .context("Failed to parse config value")?;


    println!("Value: {}", value);

    Ok(())

}
```

anyhow is ideal for applications, whereas thiserror suits libraries needing precise error control.

Panic and Unrecoverable Errors

Rust reserves panic! for unrecoverable errors. Panics will terminate the thread:

```rust
fn main() {
    panic!("Critical failure!");
}
```

Use panic! sparingly. Prefer Result and Option for errors you can recover from.

To recover from panics in special cases:

```rust
use std::panic;

fn main() {
    let result = panic::catch_unwind(|| {
        println!("This might panic");
        panic!("Boom");
    });

    match result {
        Ok(_) => println!("No panic"),
        Err(_) => println!("Recovered from panic"),
    }
}
```

This should only be used in scenarios like sandboxing or FFI.

Summary

Rust's error handling model avoids hidden control flows and encourages explicit decisions at compile time. Here are the key principles:

- Use `Option` when absence of a value is expected.

- Use `Result` when an operation may succeed or fail.

- Prefer `?` for error propagation.

- Avoid `unwrap()` and `expect()` in production unless you're certain it won't fail.

- Compose logic with `map`, `and_then`, and combinators.

- Use crates like `thiserror` and `anyhow` for larger projects.

Embracing this model leads to more predictable, safer, and maintainable Rust applications. Proper error handling isn't just about avoiding crashes—it's about making failure states explicit, discoverable, and manageable from the outset.

Chapter 5: Concurrency and Parallelism in Rust

Threads and Shared State

Concurrency is a central theme in modern software development, especially in systems programming, where maximizing the efficiency of available hardware resources is critical. Rust offers a unique take on concurrency — one that ensures memory safety and data race freedom without sacrificing performance. In this section, we'll dive deep into how Rust handles threads, how to share state safely, and how to build robust concurrent applications.

Understanding Threads

Threads allow multiple sequences of instructions to run concurrently within a program. Most modern operating systems provide threads as a unit of execution, and Rust builds on these capabilities through its standard library, offering a safe and efficient API for spawning and managing threads.

Rust uses OS threads under the hood, and the simplest way to create a new thread is with the `std::thread::spawn` function.

```
use std::thread;


fn main() {

    let handle = thread::spawn(|| {

        for i in 1..10 {

            println!("Hi from the spawned thread: {}", i);

        }

    });


    for i in 1..5 {

        println!("Hi from the main thread: {}", i);
```

```
    }


    handle.join().unwrap();

}
```

In this example, a new thread is spawned using a closure. The `join()` method blocks the main thread until the spawned thread finishes execution.

This basic example shows the power of threading, but once you start sharing data between threads, things can get complex — and dangerous — if not handled correctly.

The Problem with Shared State

Shared state between threads can lead to data races — one of the most insidious bugs in concurrent programming. A data race occurs when:

1. Two or more threads access the same memory location concurrently.

2. At least one of the accesses is a write.

3. There is no proper synchronization to coordinate the accesses.

In languages like C or C++, these bugs are hard to detect and fix. Rust, however, prevents data races at compile time by enforcing strict ownership and borrowing rules.

Ownership and Threads

Rust's ownership system extends naturally to threads. For example, if you try to move data into a thread and then use it again in the main thread, the compiler will complain unless the data implements the `Copy` trait or is otherwise properly cloned.

```
use std::thread;


fn main() {
    let message = String::from("Hello, thread!");
```

```
    let handle = thread::spawn(move || {

        println!("Message from thread: {}", message);

    });


    handle.join().unwrap();

}
```

Here, the move keyword forces the closure to take ownership of message. Once ownership is moved, message can no longer be accessed in the main thread. This ensures that no two threads can access the same data without proper synchronization.

Sharing Data Between Threads

When you do need to share state, Rust offers powerful synchronization primitives in the std::sync module, including Arc and Mutex.

Using Arc and Mutex

- Arc<T> is an atomic reference-counted pointer, allowing multiple threads to share ownership of a value.

- Mutex<T> provides mutual exclusion, ensuring that only one thread can access the data at a time.

Together, they provide safe shared mutable access to data:

```
use std::sync::{Arc, Mutex};

use std::thread;


fn main() {

    let counter = Arc::new(Mutex::new(0));

    let mut handles = vec![];
```

```
    for _ in 0..10 {

        let counter = Arc::clone(&counter);

        let handle = thread::spawn(move || {

            let mut num = counter.lock().unwrap();

            *num += 1;

        });

        handles.push(handle);

    }


    for handle in handles {

        handle.join().unwrap();

    }


    println!("Result: {}", *counter.lock().unwrap());

}
```

Here's what's happening:

- We wrap our counter in a `Mutex` to ensure mutual exclusion.

- We wrap the `Mutex` in an `Arc` to allow safe sharing between threads.

- Each thread locks the mutex, increments the counter, and releases the lock.

- After joining all threads, the final result is printed.

Without `Arc`, attempting to move the `Mutex` into multiple threads would result in a compile-time error, since `Mutex` does not implement `Copy`.

Common Mistakes and Pitfalls

Forgetting `Arc`

Trying to share a `Mutex<T>` directly between threads will not compile because `Mutex<T>` is not `Send` or `Sync` unless wrapped in `Arc`.

```rust
use std::sync::Mutex;

use std::thread;


fn main() {

    let data = Mutex::new(0);


    let handle = thread::spawn(move || {

        let mut data = data.lock().unwrap();

        *data += 1;

    });


    handle.join().unwrap();

}
```

This code will not compile because `data` is moved into the closure, and `Mutex<T>` doesn't implement `Send` for thread transfer by default. The correct approach is to wrap it in `Arc`.

Deadlocks

A common pitfall when working with mutexes is deadlocks — when two or more threads are waiting on each other to release a lock. Avoid nesting mutex locks or holding a lock across an `await` boundary in asynchronous code.

```
// Avoid holding locks for longer than necessary

let data = data.lock().unwrap();

// do the work quickly

drop(data); // explicitly release the lock
```

Always release locks as early as possible to prevent bottlenecks or deadlocks.

Thread Communication with Channels

Besides shared memory, Rust provides message-passing concurrency via channels, which allow threads to communicate safely.

```
use std::sync::mpsc;

use std::thread;

use std::time::Duration;


fn main() {

    let (tx, rx) = mpsc::channel();


    thread::spawn(move || {

        let messages = vec![

            String::from("hello"),

            String::from("from"),

            String::from("the"),

            String::from("thread"),

        ];
```

```
        for msg in messages {

            tx.send(msg).unwrap();

            thread::sleep(Duration::from_millis(500));

        }

    });


    for received in rx {

        println!("Got: {}", received);

    }

}
```

- `mpsc` stands for multiple producer, single consumer.

- `send()` transfers ownership of the message.

- The receiving end (`rx`) reads messages one at a time.

Channels are a powerful abstraction that avoids many of the pitfalls of shared state and synchronization.

Thread Pools for Efficient Concurrency

Spawning a thread per task is inefficient for large numbers of tasks. A thread pool maintains a fixed number of threads to which tasks can be submitted. The popular `rayon` crate or libraries like `tokio` for async concurrency offer thread pools.

Here's a minimal custom thread pool example:

```
use std::thread;

use std::sync::{mpsc, Arc, Mutex};
```

```rust
pub struct ThreadPool {

    workers: Vec<Worker>,

    sender: mpsc::Sender<Job>,

}


type Job = Box<dyn FnOnce() + Send + 'static>;


impl ThreadPool {

    pub fn new(size: usize) -> ThreadPool {

        let (sender, receiver) = mpsc::channel();

        let receiver = Arc::new(Mutex::new(receiver));

        let mut workers = Vec::with_capacity(size);


        for id in 0..size {

            workers.push(Worker::new(id, Arc::clone(&receiver)));

        }


        ThreadPool { workers, sender }

    }


    pub fn execute<F>(&self, f: F)

    where

        F: FnOnce() + Send + 'static,

    {
```

```
        self.sender.send(Box::new(f)).unwrap();

    }

}


struct Worker {

    id: usize,

    thread: thread::JoinHandle<()>,

}


impl Worker {

    fn new(id: usize, receiver: Arc<Mutex<mpsc::Receiver<Job>>>) ->
Worker {

        let thread = thread::spawn(move || loop {

            let job = receiver.lock().unwrap().recv().unwrap();

            println!("Worker {} got a job; executing.", id);

            job();

        });


        Worker { id, thread }

    }

}
```

This pool initializes N threads and allows task submissions using the execute method. This pattern underpins many real-world web servers and background processors.

Summary

Rust's concurrency model is unique. It blends the low-level control of C++ with compile-time guarantees that eliminate entire classes of concurrency bugs. Key takeaways:

- Use `std::thread` to spawn threads easily.

- Use `Arc` and `Mutex` together for safe shared mutable state.

- Avoid deadlocks by locking wisely and minimizing scope.

- Use channels for safe and elegant communication between threads.

- Prefer thread pools to spawning threads ad hoc for every task.

Concurrency in Rust is not only powerful but also safe by design. Once mastered, it allows you to write high-performance code that scales across cores without sacrificing reliability.

Fearless Concurrency: Mutex, Arc, and RwLock

Concurrency in Rust is not just about using threads — it's about managing shared state safely and efficiently without sacrificing performance. Rust's unique approach is often referred to as *fearless concurrency*, meaning developers can write concurrent code with confidence that the compiler will help avoid many traditional pitfalls like data races and undefined behavior. In this section, we'll go in-depth into the key primitives that enable fearless concurrency: `Mutex`, `Arc`, and `RwLock`.

Why Synchronization Primitives Matter

When multiple threads need access to shared data, synchronization is necessary to avoid corruption. Traditional languages often rely on runtime checks and hope that developers manage locks correctly, which can result in bugs that are difficult to reproduce.

Rust changes the game by pushing safety checks to compile time and making the ownership model work in harmony with concurrency. Let's examine the major synchronization tools Rust provides in its standard library.

Mutual Exclusion with `Mutex<T>`

A `Mutex` ensures that only one thread can access the data it guards at any given time. When a thread wants to access the data, it must first acquire the lock. If the lock is held by another thread, it waits (or blocks) until it can acquire the lock.

Here's a basic example of using a `Mutex`:

```
use std::sync::Mutex;


fn main() {

    let m = Mutex::new(5);


    {

        let mut num = m.lock().unwrap();

        *num += 1;

    }


    println!("m = {:?}", m);

}
```

- `Mutex::new(5)` wraps the value `5` in a mutex.

- `lock()` returns a smart pointer, `MutexGuard`, which provides safe mutable access.

- When the guard goes out of scope, the lock is automatically released.

This works well in single-threaded contexts, but when we move to multi-threading, we need to share the mutex safely.

Sharing Ownership with `Arc<T>`

Rust's ownership system ensures that only one thread owns data unless the data is wrapped in a type that explicitly allows shared ownership. `Arc<T>` (Atomic Reference Counted) enables multiple threads to own the same data safely.

Here's a practical example combining `Arc` and `Mutex`:

```rust
use std::sync::{Arc, Mutex};

use std::thread;


fn main() {

    let counter = Arc::new(Mutex::new(0));

    let mut handles = vec![];


    for _ in 0..10 {

        let counter = Arc::clone(&counter);

        let handle = thread::spawn(move || {

            let mut num = counter.lock().unwrap();

            *num += 1;

        });

        handles.push(handle);

    }


    for handle in handles {

        handle.join().unwrap();

    }


    println!("Result: {}", *counter.lock().unwrap());

}
```

Each thread increments the shared counter by acquiring a lock on the mutex. `Arc::clone` increases the reference count, allowing multiple threads to hold the mutex safely.

If you try to use `Mutex` alone without `Arc`, the compiler will complain, as `Mutex` does not implement `Send` or `Sync` by itself.

Poisoning and Handling Failures

If a thread panics while holding a mutex, the lock is considered *poisoned*, and future attempts to access it will return an error. This is a safety mechanism to prevent accessing potentially corrupted data.

You can handle poisoned mutexes gracefully:

```
let lock_result = mutex.lock();

match lock_result {

    Ok(guard) => {

        // proceed as usual

    },

    Err(poisoned) => {

        let guard = poisoned.into_inner(); // force access

        // handle with caution

    }

}
```

You should only bypass the poison error if you're confident that the data is in a valid state.

Read/Write Locking with RwLock<T>

While `Mutex<T>` allows only one thread access at a time, `RwLock<T>` (Read-Write Lock) allows multiple readers or one writer — but never both. This is more efficient when reads are frequent and writes are rare.

```rust
use std::sync::RwLock;


fn main() {

    let data = RwLock::new(5);


    {

        let r1 = data.read().unwrap();

        let r2 = data.read().unwrap();

        println!("Read locks: {}, {}", *r1, *r2);

    }


    {

        let mut w = data.write().unwrap();

        *w += 1;

    }


    println!("Final value: {}", *data.read().unwrap());

}
```

RwLock supports two methods:

- read() for acquiring a shared read lock.

- write() for acquiring an exclusive write lock.

This model can greatly improve performance in read-heavy scenarios.

Combining Arc and RwLock

Much like Mutex, if you want to share a RwLock between threads, you'll need to wrap it in an Arc.

```rust
use std::sync::{Arc, RwLock};

use std::thread;


fn main() {

    let shared_data = Arc::new(RwLock::new(vec![1, 2, 3]));


    let mut handles = vec![];


    for _ in 0..5 {

        let data = Arc::clone(&shared_data);

        handles.push(thread::spawn(move || {

            let read_guard = data.read().unwrap();

            println!("Reader thread sees: {:?}", *read_guard);

        }));

    }


    let writer = Arc::clone(&shared_data);

    handles.push(thread::spawn(move || {

        let mut write_guard = writer.write().unwrap();

        write_guard.push(4);

        println!("Writer thread updated the data");
```

```
    }));

    for handle in handles {

        handle.join().unwrap();

    }


    println!("Final data: {:?}", *shared_data.read().unwrap());

}
```

In this example:

- Multiple threads read data concurrently.

- One thread writes to it.

- The compiler and runtime enforce the rules that no reading occurs while writing and vice versa.

Deadlocks and Starvation

Even with Rust's guarantees, you can still encounter logical issues like deadlocks if you aren't careful in how you acquire locks.

```
let a = Arc::new(Mutex::new(1));

let b = Arc::new(Mutex::new(2));


let a1 = Arc::clone(&a);

let b1 = Arc::clone(&b);
```

```
let handle1 = thread::spawn(move || {

    let _a = a1.lock().unwrap();

    let _b = b1.lock().unwrap();

});


let handle2 = thread::spawn(move || {

    let _b = b.lock().unwrap();

    let _a = a.lock().unwrap();

});
```

This can lead to a deadlock if both threads lock one mutex and wait on the other. Avoid this by:

- Locking resources in a consistent order.

- Using higher-level abstractions where possible.

Starvation is another problem where one thread never gets access because others dominate the lock. Rust doesn't prevent this but using RwLock strategically can help balance access.

Interior Mutability and `RefCell`

While not directly a concurrency primitive, it's important to understand RefCell<T> provides *interior mutability* at runtime and is **not** thread-safe. It is used for single-threaded scenarios where compile-time borrowing isn't sufficient.

If you need interior mutability *and* thread safety, use Mutex<T> or RwLock<T>.

Use Cases and Patterns

Counters

Arc<Mutex<usize>> is a common pattern for shared counters across threads.

Caches

`Arc<RwLock<HashMap<K, V>>>` allows multiple readers of a cache and synchronized writes.

Thread Pools

Most Rust thread pool implementations use `Arc<Mutex<Vec<Job>>>` or a message-passing approach with channels and `Arc<Mutex<Receiver<Job>>>`.

Best Practices

- Use `Arc<Mutex<T>>` when multiple threads need mutable access to shared state.

- Use `Arc<RwLock<T>>` when multiple readers and rare writers.

- Avoid holding locks longer than necessary.

- Always handle `lock()` errors gracefully.

- Structure your code to acquire locks in consistent orders to prevent deadlocks.

- Consider using third-party libraries like `parking_lot` for more performant alternatives to `Mutex` and `RwLock`.

Summary

Rust's synchronization primitives empower developers to build safe, concurrent applications. The combination of ownership, `Arc`, `Mutex`, and `RwLock` provides a robust foundation for managing shared state across threads.

By enforcing safety at compile time and encouraging good design patterns, Rust lets you write concurrent code that is both high-performance and correct by default. When used correctly, these tools help eliminate entire classes of bugs that plague multi-threaded applications in other languages.

With fearless concurrency, you can trust that your code will scale across cores and behave predictably — no segfaults, no data races, no undefined behavior. Just safe, performant, multi-threaded Rust.

Asynchronous Programming with async/await

Modern software systems increasingly rely on non-blocking operations — whether handling HTTP requests, reading files, or communicating over networks — to maximize performance and responsiveness. Asynchronous programming addresses these needs by allowing tasks to run independently of the main execution thread. In Rust, the `async`/`await` syntax, paired with the powerful `Future` trait and asynchronous runtimes like `tokio` or `async-std`, makes writing concurrent applications expressive, efficient, and safe.

This section covers the fundamentals of async programming in Rust: what futures are, how async/await works under the hood, using async runtimes, writing concurrent and parallel tasks, and practical patterns that emerge in production systems.

The Need for Async

Blocking operations stop the entire thread from doing anything else while waiting. In synchronous programs, this limits scalability — especially in I/O-bound applications like web servers or file processors. Asynchronous programming, instead, allows the program to "pause" an operation and do something else while it waits.

Consider a synchronous file read:

```
use std::fs;


fn main() {

    let data = fs::read_to_string("file.txt").unwrap();

    println!("File contents: {}", data);

}
```

If the file is large or the disk is slow, the thread is blocked until the read completes. In an async world, this can be avoided.

Futures in Rust

At the heart of async Rust is the `Future` trait, which represents a value that may not be available yet. It is defined roughly like this:

```
pub trait Future {

    type Output;


    fn poll(self: Pin<&mut Self>, cx: &mut Context) ->
Poll<Self::Output>;

}
```

This might look complex, but it's handled automatically when you use `async` functions. Behind the scenes, `async` functions return `impl Future`.

```
async fn get_data() -> String {

    String::from("Hello, async world!")

}
```

Calling `get_data()` doesn't run the function — it returns a future that needs to be *polled* by an executor.

Using async/await

Rust's `async`/`await` syntax allows asynchronous code to be written in a way that resembles synchronous code. You mark functions as `async` and use `.await` to suspend their execution until the awaited operation is ready.

Here's a basic example using `tokio`, the most popular async runtime:

```
use tokio::time::{sleep, Duration};


#[tokio::main]

async fn main() {
```

```
println!("Waiting...");

sleep(Duration::from_secs(2)).await;

println!("Done!");
}
```

- The #[tokio::main] attribute sets up the async runtime and runs the main() function.

- sleep().await suspends the task without blocking the thread.

Building Your Own async Functions

Any function can be made asynchronous by marking it with async, and the compiler transforms it into a state machine behind the scenes.

```
async fn say_hello() {

    println!("Hello");

}
```

```
async fn greet() {

    say_hello().await;

}
```

You can chain these calls and await on them in sequence.

Concurrent Async Tasks with join!

Concurrency means running multiple operations at once. In async Rust, this is done by spawning tasks and awaiting them concurrently. The `tokio::join!` macro is useful here:

```rust
use tokio::time::{sleep, Duration};
use tokio::join;

async fn do_one() {
    sleep(Duration::from_secs(1)).await;
    println!("Finished one");
}

async fn do_two() {
    sleep(Duration::from_secs(2)).await;
    println!("Finished two");
}

#[tokio::main]
async fn main() {
    join!(do_one(), do_two());
    println!("All done");
}
```

Both tasks start at the same time, and execution resumes when both are complete.

Spawning Tasks

You can run multiple independent tasks using `tokio::spawn`, which returns a handle to the task:

```
use tokio::task;

#[tokio::main]
async fn main() {
    let handle = task::spawn(async {
        println!("Task running");
    });

    handle.await.unwrap();
}
```

Tasks spawned in this way run on the async runtime's thread pool and can operate concurrently without blocking.

Communication Between Tasks

Asynchronous code often needs communication. For this, `tokio` provides `mpsc` channels:

```
use tokio::sync::mpsc;

#[tokio::main]
async fn main() {
    let (tx, mut rx) = mpsc::channel(32);
```

```
tokio::spawn(async move {

    tx.send("hello").await.unwrap();

});


if let Some(msg) = rx.recv().await {

    println!("Got: {}", msg);

}

}
```

This works like std::sync::mpsc, but it's async-compatible and doesn't block threads.

File and Network I/O

Asynchronous I/O in Rust is non-blocking and integrated with the runtime.

Async File I/O:

```
use tokio::fs;


#[tokio::main]

async fn main() {

    let content = fs::read_to_string("file.txt").await.unwrap();

    println!("{}", content);

}
```

Async TCP Server:

```rust
use tokio::net::TcpListener;

use tokio::io::{AsyncReadExt, AsyncWriteExt};


#[tokio::main]

async fn main() -> Result<(), Box<dyn std::error::Error>> {

    let listener = TcpListener::bind("127.0.0.1:8080").await?;


    loop {

        let (mut socket, _) = listener.accept().await?;


        tokio::spawn(async move {

            let mut buf = [0; 1024];

            loop {

                let n = match socket.read(&mut buf).await {

                    Ok(n) if n == 0 => return,

                    Ok(n) => n,

                    Err(_) => return,

                };


                if socket.write_all(&buf[0..n]).await.is_err() {

                    return;

                }

            }

        });
```

```
        }

}
```

This echo server:

- Listens on a TCP socket.

- Accepts incoming connections.

- Reads and writes asynchronously.

Working with `select!`

`select!` allows you to await multiple futures and proceed with whichever completes first:

```rust
use tokio::time::{sleep, Duration};
use tokio::select;


#[tokio::main]
async fn main() {
    let a = sleep(Duration::from_secs(1));
    let b = sleep(Duration::from_secs(2));

    select! {
        _ = a => println!("A finished first"),
        _ = b => println!("B finished first"),
    }
}
```

This is useful for timeouts, fallbacks, and racing tasks.

Cancellation and Timeouts

Async tasks can be cancelled automatically if their future is dropped. You can also use `tokio::time::timeout` to control execution time:

```rust
use tokio::time::{timeout, Duration};

#[tokio::main]
async fn main() {
    let result = timeout(Duration::from_secs(1), async {
        // long task
        tokio::time::sleep(Duration::from_secs(2)).await;
        "done"
    }).await;

    match result {
        Ok(msg) => println!("Success: {}", msg),
        Err(_) => println!("Timed out!"),
    }
}
```

Error Handling in Async Code

Async functions can return `Result<T, E>` just like sync functions. Use `?` to propagate errors.

```rust
async fn might_fail() -> Result<(), Box<dyn std::error::Error>> {

    let data = tokio::fs::read_to_string("missing.txt").await?;

    println!("{}", data);

    Ok(())

}
```

If the file doesn't exist, the error propagates, and the caller can handle it.

Writing Custom Executors (Advanced)

Executors are responsible for polling and scheduling futures. While you usually use `tokio` or `async-std`, you can build a simple one:

```rust
use std::future::Future;

use std::pin::Pin;

use std::task::{Context, Poll, Waker};

use std::thread;

use std::time::Duration;

use futures::task::noop_waker;


fn block_on<F: Future>(mut future: F) -> F::Output {

    let waker = noop_waker();

    let mut context = Context::from_waker(&waker);

    let mut pinned = unsafe { Pin::new_unchecked(&mut future) };
```

```
    loop {

        match pinned.as_mut().poll(&mut context) {

            Poll::Ready(val) => return val,

            Poll::Pending =>
thread::sleep(Duration::from_millis(10)),

        }

    }

}
```

This is for learning purposes — in production, always use mature runtimes.

Best Practices

- Prefer `async` over threads for I/O-heavy tasks.

- Use `tokio::spawn` for fire-and-forget tasks.

- Be careful not to block within async code (no `std::thread::sleep`!).

- Use structured concurrency to ensure tasks don't outlive their context.

- Avoid unnecessary `.await` inside loops — use `FuturesUnordered` for bulk task execution.

Summary

Async programming in Rust provides powerful tools to write high-performance, scalable applications. With `async`/`await`, you can describe complex asynchronous operations cleanly and expressively, while the compiler guarantees memory and concurrency safety.

By embracing futures, async I/O, task spawning, and synchronization primitives, you can confidently build applications ranging from web servers and microservices to real-time systems — all without falling into the traps of traditional concurrency. Rust's async model allows you to think sequentially, write declaratively, and scale efficiently — the hallmark of fearless asynchronous programming.

Real-World Concurrent Rust Applications

Building concurrent applications in the real world demands more than just a solid understanding of `threads`, `async`, or `mutexes` — it requires practical design, careful resource management, error handling, and performance tuning. Rust's model of fearless concurrency isn't merely theoretical; it shines in actual production systems, where memory safety and concurrency correctness are critical. This section explores how concurrency is applied in complete systems, including server architectures, task scheduling, background processing, and reactive event-driven applications.

Designing Concurrent Architectures in Rust

Real-world concurrent systems often involve multiple layers and responsibilities:

- **IO-bound tasks**: Network requests, file reads, and database interactions.

- **CPU-bound tasks**: Parsing, transformation, and computation.

- **Scheduling**: Coordinating tasks without blocking.

- **Error propagation and resilience**: Systems must recover gracefully.

Rust offers the primitives to build each of these with clarity and correctness. The two main concurrency paradigms in real-world Rust applications are:

- **Multi-threading with synchronization** (using `Arc`, `Mutex`, `RwLock`)

- **Async task-based concurrency** (with `tokio`, `async-std`, `smol`)

Choosing between them depends on the nature of the problem — whether it's I/O-heavy or compute-heavy.

Building a Concurrent Web Server

Let's consider building a basic concurrent web server. We'll use `tokio` for its async I/O model and `hyper` for HTTP handling.

```
use hyper::{Body, Request, Response, Server};

use hyper::service::{make_service_fn, service_fn};

use std::convert::Infallible;


async fn handle(req: Request<Body>) -> Result<Response<Body>,
Infallible> {

    Ok(Response::new(Body::from("Hello, concurrent world!")))

}


#[tokio::main]

async fn main() {

    let make_svc = make_service_fn(|_conn| async {

        Ok::<_, Infallible>(service_fn(handle))

    });


    let addr = ([127, 0, 0, 1], 3000).into();


    let server = Server::bind(&addr).serve(make_svc);


    println!("Server running on http://{}", addr);

    if let Err(e) = server.await {

        eprintln!("Server error: {}", e);

    }

}
```

Each connection is handled asynchronously. This server can manage thousands of simultaneous connections without needing thousands of threads.

Database Access with Concurrency

Accessing databases concurrently is a core requirement for web apps, APIs, and data services. Libraries like `sqlx` or `diesel` provide async-compatible clients.

```rust
use sqlx::postgres::PgPoolOptions;


#[tokio::main]

async fn main() -> Result<(), sqlx::Error> {

    let pool = PgPoolOptions::new()

        .max_connections(5)

        .connect("postgres://user:pass@localhost/mydb")

        .await?;


    let row: (i32,) = sqlx::query_as("SELECT 1")

        .fetch_one(&pool)

        .await?;


    println!("Query result: {}", row.0);


    Ok(())

}
```

Using a connection pool allows multiple tasks to query the database concurrently without blocking.

Background Workers and Job Queues

Rust is excellent for background processing and job scheduling. You might have tasks that:

- Resize images

- Send emails

- Process logs

- Analyze data streams

Let's simulate a background job queue using `tokio::sync::mpsc`:

```rust
use tokio::sync::mpsc;
use tokio::time::{sleep, Duration};


#[derive(Debug)]
enum Job {
    Email(String),
    ResizeImage(String),
}


async fn worker(mut rx: mpsc::Receiver<Job>) {
    while let Some(job) = rx.recv().await {
        match job {
            Job::Email(to) => {
                println!("Sending email to {}", to);
```

```
            sleep(Duration::from_secs(1)).await;

        },

        Job::ResizeImage(img) => {

            println!("Resizing image {}", img);

            sleep(Duration::from_secs(2)).await;

        },

    }

  }

}


#[tokio::main]

async fn main() {

    let (tx, rx) = mpsc::channel(32);


    tokio::spawn(worker(rx));


    tx.send(Job::Email("user@example.com".into())).await.unwrap();

    tx.send(Job::ResizeImage("pic.jpg".into())).await.unwrap();


    sleep(Duration::from_secs(5)).await;

}
```

This model scales well — you can spawn multiple workers and balance load across them.

Real-Time Event-Driven Systems

In many real-world systems (IoT, financial tickers, games), you must handle streams of events. Rust's `tokio::sync::broadcast` or `tokio_stream` crates allow you to model pub-sub patterns.

```rust
use tokio::sync::broadcast;

use tokio_stream::wrappers::BroadcastStream;

use tokio_stream::StreamExt;


#[tokio::main]

async fn main() {

    let (tx, _) = broadcast::channel(16);


    let mut reader = BroadcastStream::new(tx.subscribe());


    tokio::spawn(async move {

        for i in 0..5 {

            tx.send(format!("Event {}", i)).unwrap();

tokio::time::sleep(tokio::time::Duration::from_millis(500)).await;

        }

    });


    while let Some(Ok(msg)) = reader.next().await {

        println!("Received: {}", msg);

    }
```

```
}
```

Multiple consumers can subscribe to the broadcast stream. This is essential in reactive applications like dashboards, multiplayer games, or telemetry systems.

Parallelism with Rayon

While async is ideal for I/O, CPU-bound operations benefit from true parallelism. The `rayon` crate offers an ergonomic parallel iterator API:

```rust
use rayon::prelude::*;

fn main() {
    let data: Vec<u64> = (0..1_000_000).collect();

    let sum: u64 = data.par_iter().map(|x| x * 2).sum();

    println!("Parallel sum: {}", sum);
}
```

Rayon automatically distributes the workload across available CPU cores, providing massive speedups with minimal effort.

Metrics, Logging, and Observability

Concurrency introduces complexity. Observability becomes essential. Real-world Rust applications often integrate with:

- `tracing`: Structured async-aware logging.

- `metrics`: Emitting counters, histograms, etc.

- `tokio-console`: Visualizing async tasks in development.

Example with `tracing`:

```
use tracing::{info, instrument};
use tracing_subscriber;


#[instrument]
async fn process_job(id: u32) {
    info!("Started job");
    tokio::time::sleep(tokio::time::Duration::from_secs(1)).await;
    info!("Finished job");
}


#[tokio::main]
async fn main() {
    tracing_subscriber::fmt::init();

    let handles: Vec<_> = (1..=5)
        .map(|id| tokio::spawn(process_job(id)))
        .collect();

    for handle in handles {
        handle.await.unwrap();
```

```
    }

}
```

This structured log output includes span contexts and makes debugging easier.

Handling Failures Gracefully

In real-world systems, concurrency should be resilient. When a task fails:

- You might want to retry.

- You might want to log and recover.

- You might need to restart a whole subsystem.

Rust's strong type system helps you propagate and manage errors at every level.

Here's a retry pattern using a simple loop:

```rust
async fn do_work() -> Result<(), String> {

    Err("Temporary failure".into())

}


#[tokio::main]

async fn main() {

    for attempt in 1..=3 {

        match do_work().await {

            Ok(_) => {

                println!("Success");

                break;
```

```
                }

            Err(e) => {

                println!("Attempt {} failed: {}", attempt, e);

tokio::time::sleep(tokio::time::Duration::from_secs(1)).await;

            }

        }

    }

}
```

Libraries like `retry`, `tower`, or `backoff` offer more advanced patterns.

Microservices and Distributed Systems

In distributed Rust systems, each service might run independently and communicate over HTTP, gRPC, or message queues. `axum`, `tonic`, and `nats.rs` are common building blocks.

For example, using `axum` for a concurrent REST API:

```
use axum::{Router, routing::get, response::IntoResponse};


async fn hello() -> impl IntoResponse {

    "Hello from async Rust"

}


#[tokio::main]

async fn main() {
```

```rust
let app = Router::new().route("/", get(hello));

axum::Server::bind(&"127.0.0.1:3000".parse().unwrap())

    .serve(app.into_make_service())

    .await

    .unwrap();

}
```

This can scale across threads, cores, or containers with predictable performance and no memory safety concerns.

Lessons from the Field

From embedded controllers to cloud-native services, here are a few lessons observed from large Rust codebases:

- **Use structured concurrency**: Keep spawned tasks scoped and join them explicitly.

- **Avoid mixing sync and async**: Blocking calls inside async functions will hinder performance.

- **Prefer message passing for complex coordination**: Channels reduce lock contention.

- **Use high-level crates**: Don't reinvent thread pools or retry logic unless necessary.

- **Instrument everything**: Use tracing and metrics early — debugging concurrency is hard without visibility.

Summary

Concurrency in the real world is about more than correctness — it's about maintainability, performance, observability, and fault tolerance. Rust's concurrency model offers a pragmatic and safe way to build modern software systems that are robust and performant from the ground up.

Whether you're building a web server, a parallel data processing pipeline, a microservice, or an event-driven system, Rust gives you the tools to model concurrency cleanly, scale confidently, and avoid the subtle bugs that plague traditional systems. By applying the patterns and practices in this chapter, you can write real-world concurrent Rust that is fast, reliable, and production-ready.

Chapter 6: Advanced Rust: Macros, Traits, and Metaprogramming

Understanding and Writing Rust Macros

Macros in Rust are a powerful metaprogramming feature that enable developers to write more concise, reusable, and efficient code. Unlike functions, which operate on values, macros operate on the abstract syntax tree (AST) of the code itself. This allows macros to generate and manipulate code at compile time, providing capabilities that functions cannot match.

Rust supports two main types of macros: **declarative macros** (also known as "macro_rules!") and **procedural macros**. Declarative macros use pattern matching to transform code, while procedural macros operate on the Rust syntax tree using code written in Rust itself. Both forms of macros enable powerful abstractions that enhance expressiveness, reduce boilerplate, and improve code clarity when used appropriately.

The Need for Macros

Rust is a statically typed language with strong safety guarantees, but this can sometimes lead to verbose code. Macros provide a way to remove repetitive patterns without sacrificing type safety. For example, logging, assertions, and conditional compilation are common use cases for macros.

Rust's standard library itself heavily relies on macros like `println!`, `vec!`, `format!`, and `assert!`. Understanding how to write your own macros gives you access to similar capabilities for your custom logic.

Declarative Macros (`macro_rules!`)

Declarative macros allow developers to define macros using a simple pattern-matching syntax. Let's start with a basic example.

```
macro_rules! say_hello {

    () => {

        println!("Hello!");

    };
```

```
}
```

This macro, `say_hello!`, takes no arguments and expands to a `println!` invocation. To use it:

```
fn main() {

    say_hello!(); // Outputs: Hello!

}
```

Matching Patterns with Arguments

You can also define macros that accept arguments:

```
macro_rules! greet {

    ($name:expr) => {

        println!("Hello, {}!", $name);

    };

}
```

Here, $name:expr tells the macro to match any Rust expression and bind it to the variable $name. This enables flexibility in input:

```
fn main() {

    greet!("Alice");

    greet!(format!("Mr. {}", "Smith"));

}
```

Matching Multiple Patterns

Declarative macros can also support multiple patterns:

```
macro_rules! compute {
    ($a:expr + $b:expr) => {
        println!("Sum: {}", $a + $b);
    };
    ($a:expr * $b:expr) => {
        println!("Product: {}", $a * $b);
    };
}
```

This macro allows both addition and multiplication patterns:

```
fn main() {
    compute!(3 + 4);
    compute!(3 * 4);
}
```

This kind of macro can help model simple DSLs (domain-specific languages) or operator overloading syntaxes.

Repetition in Macros

Rust macros support repetition with $(...), * constructs. For example, let's build a macro to define multiple variables at once:

```
macro_rules! define_vars {

    ($($name:ident = $value:expr);*) => {

        $(

            let $name = $value;

        )*

    };

}
```

Usage:

```
fn main() {

    define_vars! {

        x = 10;

        y = 20;

        z = 30

    };


    println!("x = {}, y = {}, z = {}", x, y, z);

}
```

This is a major win when you need to generate multiple items from a repetitive pattern.

Procedural Macros

Procedural macros are more complex but also more powerful. Unlike `macro_rules!`, procedural macros allow developers to manipulate the Rust AST programmatically. These macros come in three main forms:

1. **Custom Derive Macros**

2. **Attribute-like Macros**

3. **Function-like Macros**

Procedural macros must be defined in their own crate with `proc-macro = true` in `Cargo.toml`.

Custom Derive Macros

These are used to automatically implement traits for types. For instance:

```
#[derive(Debug)]

struct Point {

    x: i32,

    y: i32,

}
```

To create a custom derive macro:

1. Create a new crate:

```
cargo new my_macro --lib
```

In `Cargo.toml` of `my_macro`:

```
[lib]

proc-macro = true
```

In `lib.rs`:

```
extern crate proc_macro;

use proc_macro::TokenStream;

#[proc_macro_derive(MyDebug)]
pub fn my_debug_derive(input: TokenStream) -> TokenStream {
    // Parse and generate code
    // Here we would usually use the `syn` and `quote` crates.
    unimplemented!()
}
```

To implement the full version, you'd typically include:

```
syn = "2.0"
quote = "1.0"
```

This lets you parse the input and generate tokens safely and ergonomically.

Attribute-like Macros

These macros look like custom attributes and are used for code modification or metadata handling.

Example:

```
#[route(GET, "/")]
```

```
fn index() {

    // ...

}
```

You can define this similarly to custom derives, but with `#[proc_macro_attribute]`.

Function-like Macros

These look like regular function calls but operate on tokens:

```
html! {

    <div>

        <p>"Hello, world!"</p>

    </div>

}
```

They're commonly used in frameworks like Yew for React-style JSX in Rust.

Hygiene and Scoping in Macros

Rust macros maintain **hygiene**, meaning they don't accidentally override or interfere with variables outside their scope. This avoids subtle bugs and name collisions.

```
macro_rules! hygiene_example {

    () => {

        let x = 100;

        println!("Inside macro: {}", x);
```

```
    };

}


fn main() {

    let x = 50;

    hygiene_example!();

    println!("Outside macro: {}", x);

}
```

Even though x is declared inside the macro, it doesn't affect the outer x. This scoping principle is vital for safe macro usage.

Debugging Macros

Debugging macros can be challenging since they expand during compilation. Use the following tools:

- `cargo expand` (via `cargo install cargo-expand`) to see the expanded code.

- Compiler errors will often show the macro backtrace.

- Avoid deeply nested or cryptic macros.

Macro Best Practices

- **Keep them readable**: Use meaningful pattern names and comments.

- **Use only when necessary**: Prefer functions, traits, or generics for simpler tasks.

- **Test macro behavior**: Use unit tests and expanded output to verify correctness.

- **Avoid macros that obscure intent**: Clear code is better than clever code.

Real-World Examples

Logging Macro

```rust
macro_rules! log_info {

    ($($arg:tt)*) => {

        println!("[INFO]: {}", format!($($arg)*));

    };

}
```

Usage:

```rust
fn main() {

    log_info!("User {} logged in at {}", "Alice", "12:00 PM");

}
```

Implementing a DSL

```rust
macro_rules! html {

    (<$tag:ident>$($inner:tt)*</$tag2:ident>) => {

        {

            assert_eq!(stringify!($tag), stringify!($tag2));

            format!("<{0}>{1}</{0}>", stringify!($tag),
html!($($inner)*))

        }
```

```
    };

    ($text:expr) => {

        $text.to_string()

    };

}


fn main() {

    let html_code = html!(

        <div>

            <p>"Welcome"</p>

        </div>

    );


    println!("{}", html_code); // <div><p>Welcome</p></div>

}
```

This example shows how Rust macros can implement a basic HTML templating DSL, turning syntax into valid HTML strings.

Summary

Macros in Rust are powerful tools that allow compile-time code generation, abstraction, and minimization of boilerplate. Declarative macros are simple and powerful for pattern matching, while procedural macros give you fine-grained control over code generation by manipulating Rust's AST.

While macros can greatly improve code reuse and flexibility, they should be used judiciously. Overuse or misuse can lead to unreadable and hard-to-debug code. However, when used well, macros elevate Rust's expressive power, enabling safe and performant abstractions in systems-level programming.

Using Traits for Abstraction

Traits are one of Rust's core abstraction mechanisms, allowing you to define shared behavior across different types. Traits are similar to interfaces in other languages, but more powerful and flexible in how they interact with Rust's ownership model, lifetimes, and generics.

At their heart, traits are contracts: they define functionality a type must provide if it implements the trait. This enables polymorphism in Rust, both static (at compile time using generics) and dynamic (via trait objects). By mastering traits, you unlock the power to build reusable, modular, and type-safe abstractions in your systems code.

Defining and Implementing Traits

Let's begin by defining a simple trait:

```
trait Greet {

    fn greet(&self) -> String;

}
```

This trait specifies that any type implementing Greet must provide a greet method that returns a String.

Now we can implement this trait for a struct:

```
struct Person {

    name: String,

}
```

```
impl Greet for Person {

    fn greet(&self) -> String {

        format!("Hello, my name is {}.", self.name)
```

```
    }

}
```

Usage:

```
fn main() {

    let p = Person { name: String::from("Alice") };

    println!("{}", p.greet());

}
```

Traits can be implemented for any type, including built-in types and types you don't own using the **newtype pattern**.

Default Trait Implementations

Traits can also provide default method implementations. This allows types to only override behavior when they need to:

```
trait Printable {

    fn print(&self) {

        println!("Default print.");

    }

}
```

Types can then either use the default:

```
struct Unit;
```

```
impl Printable for Unit {}
```

Or override it:

```
struct Custom;
```

```
impl Printable for Custom {

    fn print(&self) {

        println!("Custom print.");

    }

}
```

Traits and Generics

Traits are closely tied to Rust's generic system. You can use traits as **bounds** on generic types:

```
fn print_greeting<T: Greet>(item: T) {

    println!("{}", item.greet());

}
```

Or with multiple traits:

```
fn do_something<T: Greet + Printable>(item: T) {
```

```
    item.print();

    println!("{}", item.greet());

}
```

This is known as trait-bound polymorphism. The compiler generates specialized code for each concrete type used with a generic function, offering zero-cost abstraction.

You can also use a **where clause** for cleaner syntax:

```
fn do_other<T>(item: T)

where

    T: Greet + Printable,

{

    item.print();

    println!("{}", item.greet());

}
```

Trait Objects and Dynamic Dispatch

Sometimes you don't know the concrete type at compile time, or you want to work with heterogeneous collections. That's where **trait objects** come in, enabling dynamic dispatch.

```
fn greet_dynamic(person: &dyn Greet) {

    println!("{}", person.greet());

}
```

This works because `&dyn Greet` is a fat pointer — it contains a pointer to the data and a pointer to a vtable (a virtual method table). This allows method calls to be resolved at runtime.

Example:

```
let p = Person { name: String::from("Bob") };

greet_dynamic(&p);
```

You can also store trait objects in vectors:

```
let items: Vec<Box<dyn Greet>> = vec![

    Box::new(Person { name: "Alice".into() }),

    Box::new(Person { name: "Bob".into() }),

];
```

Then iterate:

```
for item in items.iter() {

    println!("{}", item.greet());

}
```

Note that trait objects require the trait to be **object safe**, which means:

- All methods must return `Self` or types not involving `Self` (except in the receiver, e.g., `&self` is fine).

- They must not have generic parameters.

Associated Functions and Constants

Traits can define associated functions and constants, which are useful for shared behavior or metadata:

```rust
trait Identifiable {

    const ID: &'static str;


    fn id(&self) -> &'static str {

        Self::ID

    }

}


struct Device;


impl Identifiable for Device {

    const ID: &'static str = "device_001";

}
```

Usage:

```rust
let dev = Device;

println!("ID: {}", dev.id());
```

Blanket Implementations

One of Rust's most powerful features is the ability to write **blanket implementations** — trait implementations for all types satisfying certain conditions:

```
trait Hello {

    fn say_hello(&self);

}
```

```
impl<T: std::fmt::Display> Hello for T {

    fn say_hello(&self) {

        println!("Hello, {}!", self);

    }

}
```

Now any type that implements `Display` also gets `say_hello()` for free:

```
fn main() {

    let name = "Rust";

    name.say_hello(); // Hello, Rust!

}
```

This promotes maximum code reuse without boilerplate.

Supertraits

Sometimes a trait depends on another. This is where **supertraits** come in.

```
trait Displayable: std::fmt::Display {

    fn display_twice(&self) {

        println!("{} {}", self, self);

    }

}
```

Since `Displayable` requires `Display`, you can use formatting syntax within the method.

You can implement this as:

```
impl Displayable for i32 {}
```

Now:

```
fn main() {

    42.display_twice(); // 42 42

}
```

Supertraits create powerful hierarchies and ensure capabilities are present before providing functionality.

Trait Inheritance and Composition

You can compose behavior by combining multiple traits:

```
trait Readable {

    fn read(&self) -> String;

}
```

```rust
trait Writable {

    fn write(&mut self, data: &str);

}


trait IO: Readable + Writable {}


struct File;


impl Readable for File {

    fn read(&self) -> String {

        String::from("file content")

    }

}


impl Writable for File {

    fn write(&mut self, data: &str) {

        println!("Writing: {}", data);

    }

}


impl IO for File {}
```

This mimics inheritance hierarchies, but with full control and explicitness. It avoids the pitfalls of traditional OOP inheritance.

Traits vs. Inheritance

Rust's trait system offers many of the benefits of inheritance without its downsides:

Feature	Traits	Classical Inheritance
Multiple abstraction	✓ (via trait bounds and impls)	✗ (most languages support only single inheritance)
Type safety	✓	Depends on language
Zero-cost abstraction	✓	✗ (often involves runtime cost)
Extensibility	✓ (traits can be added externally)	✗ (requires altering base classes)
Dynamic dispatch	✓ (opt-in via trait objects)	✓

Rust's trait system encourages composition over inheritance, leading to cleaner and more maintainable designs.

Traits and Lifetimes

Traits can also be parameterized by lifetimes, especially when returning references:

```
trait Description {
    fn describe(&self) -> &str;
```

```
}
```

This is fine when the returned reference has the same lifetime as `self`. But for more complex relationships, you can add explicit lifetimes:

```
trait Description<'a> {

    fn describe(&'a self) -> &'a str;

}
```

This is mostly needed in generic code where the compiler can't infer lifetimes.

Trait Bounds in Structs and Enums

You can use trait bounds in generic structs:

```
struct Wrapper<T: Greet> {

    item: T,

}


impl<T: Greet> Wrapper<T> {

    fn greet_item(&self) {

        println!("{}", self.item.greet());

    }

}
```

This ensures that `Wrapper<T>` is only valid for types that implement `Greet`.

You can also store trait objects if dynamic behavior is required:

```
struct BoxedWrapper {

    item: Box<dyn Greet>,

}
```

Trait Derivation and #[derive]

Rust allows automatic trait implementations using the #[derive(...)] attribute. Common derived traits include:

- Debug

- Clone

- PartialEq

- Eq

- Ord

- Hash

- Default

Example:

```
#[derive(Debug, Clone, PartialEq)]

struct Point {

    x: i32,

    y: i32,

}
```

You can derive your own traits using **procedural macros**, as covered in the previous section.

Summary

Traits are essential to idiomatic Rust. They allow you to define shared behavior, abstract over types, and build safe, reusable, and composable code. Rust's trait system strikes a balance between flexibility and type safety, supporting both compile-time polymorphism through generics and runtime polymorphism through trait objects.

Key takeaways:

- Traits define shared behavior and can have default implementations.

- Generics with trait bounds enable static polymorphism.

- Trait objects (`dyn Trait`) enable dynamic polymorphism.

- Blanket implementations and supertraits empower flexible abstractions.

- Traits support composability, testability, and zero-cost abstractions.

Mastering traits is crucial for advanced Rust development, especially in systems programming where performance, safety, and abstraction must coexist without compromise.

Advanced Type Features: Associated Types, GATs, and Dyn Traits

Rust's type system is one of its defining features—offering both power and precision. In this section, we dive deep into some of its most advanced capabilities: **associated types**, **generic associated types (GATs)**, and **dyn traits**. These features enable expressive abstractions, elegant generic code, and flexible trait design, all while preserving Rust's commitment to zero-cost abstractions and strong safety guarantees.

Associated Types

Associated types are a mechanism to define placeholder types within a trait. Instead of requiring every implementer to specify generic type parameters directly, the trait itself declares associated types that can be filled in during implementation. This improves readability and ergonomics for complex generic code.

Basic Example

Let's start by defining a trait with an associated type:

```
trait Iterator {

    type Item;


    fn next(&mut self) -> Option<Self::Item>;

}
```

This is similar to the standard `Iterator` trait in the Rust standard library. The `Item` type is associated with the trait and gets resolved when the trait is implemented.

```
struct Counter {

    count: usize,

}


impl Iterator for Counter {

    type Item = usize;


    fn next(&mut self) -> Option<Self::Item> {

        self.count += 1;

        if self.count <= 5 {

            Some(self.count)

        } else {

            None
```

```
        }

    }

}
```

This design enables implementations to bind to a concrete `Item` type without forcing generic type arguments on all consumers of the trait.

```rust
fn print_all<I: Iterator>(mut iter: I) {

    while let Some(value) = iter.next() {

        println!("{}", value);

    }

}
```

Associated Types vs Generics

You may ask: Why use associated types when you can use generics?

```rust
trait MyTrait<T> {

    fn do_something(&self, value: T);

}
```

vs.

```rust
trait MyTrait {

    type Value;
```

```
    fn do_something(&self, value: Self::Value);

}
```

Associated types allow cleaner method signatures, especially when multiple methods within a trait use the same type.

Generics, on the other hand, allow a single trait to be implemented multiple times for different types. For example:

```
impl MyTrait<u32> for MyType { ... }

impl MyTrait<String> for MyType { ... }
```

So the choice depends on whether you want multiple implementations per type (`<T>`) or a single cohesive trait definition (`type Value`).

Associated Types in Complex Traits

Let's take an example from parsing.

```
trait Parse {

    type Output;


    fn parse(&self, input: &str) -> Result<Self::Output, String>;

}
```

This allows different parsers to produce different output types:

```
struct IntParser;
```

```rust
impl Parse for IntParser {

    type Output = i32;


    fn parse(&self, input: &str) -> Result<Self::Output, String> {

        input.parse::<i32>().map_err(|_| "Failed to parse
int".into())

    }

}


struct BoolParser;


impl Parse for BoolParser {

    type Output = bool;


    fn parse(&self, input: &str) -> Result<Self::Output, String> {

        input.parse::<bool>().map_err(|_| "Failed to parse
bool".into())

    }

}
```

Using associated types keeps your APIs clean while supporting expressive implementations.

Generic Associated Types (GATs)

Generic Associated Types (GATs) are a powerful extension of associated types. They allow you to declare associated types that themselves take generic parameters. This unlocks a large class of patterns previously impossible or extremely awkward in Rust.

The Problem GATs Solve

Let's say you have a trait that produces some kind of reference:

```
trait Lender {

    type Loan<'a>;



    fn lend<'a>(&'a self) -> Self::Loan<'a>;

}
```

In this example, the associated type Loan is generic over 'a. Without GATs, this kind of expression is not possible—you couldn't express lifetimes or type parameters within associated types. GATs lift this restriction.

This allows writing container-like traits with references to internal data:

```
struct LendingVec<T> {

    data: Vec<T>,

}


impl<T> Lender for LendingVec<T> {

    type Loan<'a> = &'a [T];



    fn lend<'a>(&'a self) -> Self::Loan<'a> {

        &self.data

    }
```

```
}
```

This is powerful because it enables APIs where borrowed data can be modeled cleanly using associated types and lifetimes together.

Practical GAT Example

Let's build a trait for collections that can yield temporary views into their elements:

```
trait Viewable {

    type View<'a>

    where

        Self: 'a;


    fn view<'a>(&'a self) -> Self::View<'a>;
}
```

This allows containers to expose a temporary "window" of their contents:

```
struct Container {

    items: Vec<String>,

}


impl Viewable for Container {

    type View<'a> = &'a [String];
```

```
fn view<'a>(&'a self) -> Self::View<'a> {

    &self.items

}

}
```

Without GATs, you would need to define View for a fixed lifetime, which is brittle and limits composability. GATs eliminate this problem by tying the lifetime directly to the trait method context.

GATs are especially important in areas like async programming, streaming, parsing, and borrowed iterators.

---

dyn Trait and Trait Objects

The dyn keyword introduces a **trait object**, a form of dynamic dispatch in Rust. It allows the use of trait references at runtime without knowing the underlying concrete type at compile time.

```
fn print_trait(obj: &dyn std::fmt::Display) {

    println!("{}", obj);

}
```

You can use dyn Trait for functions, structs, and collections:

```
let things: Vec<Box<dyn std::fmt::Display>> = vec![

    Box::new(42),

    Box::new("hello"),

    Box::new(3.14),

];
```

Each item can be treated polymorphically, as long as it implements the required trait.

When to Use dyn

Use dyn Trait when:

- You need heterogeneous types in a collection.

- You want to defer type decisions to runtime.

- The abstraction requires dynamic extensibility.

Avoid dyn when:

- You need performance-critical code (static dispatch is faster).

- You want to avoid heap allocation.

- The trait is not object-safe.

Object Safety and Limitations

Not all traits can be turned into trait objects. Traits must satisfy **object safety**:

- Methods must not use Self in return types.

- Methods must not be generic.

For example, this is **not** object-safe:

```
trait MyTrait {
    fn create() -> Self;
}
```

But this **is**:

```
trait MyTrait {

    fn print(&self);

}
```

Why? Because the first trait uses `Self` in a way that the compiler can't resolve dynamically. Trait objects require methods that can be called uniformly through a vtable.

Trait Upcasting (Experimental)

Trait upcasting is a proposed feature that allows treating one trait object as another if one is a supertrait of the other:

```
trait A {}

trait B: A {}
```

```
fn use_a(obj: &dyn B) {

    let base: &dyn A = obj;

}
```

Currently, this feature is available behind a compiler flag. Once stabilized, it will improve ergonomics for layered trait hierarchies.

Advanced: Self-Referential Types with GATs

GATs help model self-referential types more cleanly. Let's consider a parser that yields elements from a buffer:

```
trait Parser {
```

```
type Item<'a>

where

    Self: 'a;



fn parse<'a>(&'a mut self) -> Option<Self::Item<'a>>;

}
```

This kind of design was previously impossible, as you couldn't express that `Item` has a lifetime tied to `self`. With GATs, you can now do this in a robust and idiomatic way.

This is particularly useful in async iterators, streaming protocols, and resource pools where temporality is core to the abstraction.

Summary

Rust's advanced type features give developers incredible power to build elegant and performant systems. These include:

- **Associated Types**: Provide type placeholders in traits, reducing boilerplate and improving readability.

- **Generic Associated Types (GATs)**: Extend associated types to be generic, enabling flexible lifetimes and richer abstractions.

- `dyn` **Traits**: Enable dynamic dispatch and runtime polymorphism, useful for plugin systems and heterogeneous collections.

These features allow for precise and flexible APIs, enabling traits to model complex relationships and lifetimes. They also facilitate abstractions common in systems programming—without giving up on safety or zero-cost guarantees. Mastering them is key to harnessing Rust's full potential in designing robust, reusable, and high-performance software.

Metaprogramming and Code Generation

Metaprogramming in Rust refers to the ability to write programs that generate or manipulate code at compile time. This can lead to more expressive, reusable, and performant abstractions. While Rust doesn't support traditional macros like C or Lisp (which manipulate raw text), it provides **hygienic macros**, **procedural macros**, and **build scripts** that together form a powerful metaprogramming toolkit.

Rust's approach ensures correctness and maintainability by integrating metaprogramming directly into the type system and compilation process. In this section, we will explore various metaprogramming tools in Rust, their use cases, and real-world examples.

Declarative Macros Recap

Declarative macros (`macro_rules!`) are the foundation of metaprogramming in Rust. They operate using pattern matching and substitution.

Example:

```
macro_rules! repeat {

    ($val:expr, $n:expr) => {{

        let mut vec = Vec::new();

        for _ in 0..$n {

            vec.push($val);

        }

        vec

    }};

}


fn main() {

    let nums = repeat!(5, 3); // [5, 5, 5]

}
```

They are powerful for reducing boilerplate and expressing repeatable patterns but are limited when you need more logic or want to inspect types or structures.

Procedural Macros

Procedural macros offer fine-grained control over code generation. They allow developers to write functions that accept and return Rust code as token streams. These macros operate on the abstract syntax tree (AST) and are ideal for advanced metaprogramming needs.

There are three types:

1. **Custom derive**: `#[derive(...)]`

2. **Attribute-like**: `#[my_attr]`

3. **Function-like**: `my_macro!(...)`

Procedural macros live in a separate crate with `proc-macro = true` in `Cargo.toml`.

Creating a Procedural Macro

Let's walk through creating a custom derive macro.

Step 1: Create a new crate

```
cargo new my_macros --lib
```

In `my_macros/Cargo.toml`:

```
[lib]
proc-macro = true


[dependencies]
syn = "2.0"
quote = "1.0"
```

Step 2: Write the macro

In `lib.rs`:

```rust
extern crate proc_macro;

use proc_macro::TokenStream;

use quote::quote;

use syn::{parse_macro_input, DeriveInput};


#[proc_macro_derive(HelloMacro)]

pub fn hello_macro_derive(input: TokenStream) -> TokenStream {

    let input = parse_macro_input!(input as DeriveInput);

    let name = &input.ident;


    let expanded = quote! {

        impl HelloMacro for #name {

            fn hello() {

                println!("Hello from {}!", stringify!(#name));

            }

        }

    };


    TokenStream::from(expanded)

}
```

Step 3: Use the macro

In another crate:

```
[dependencies]

my_macros = { path = "../my_macros" }
```

```
use my_macros::HelloMacro;
```

```
#[derive(HelloMacro)]

struct MyStruct;
```

```
trait HelloMacro {

    fn hello();

}
```

```
fn main() {

    MyStruct::hello(); // Prints: Hello from MyStruct!

}
```

This demonstrates code generation based on structural input. This pattern is common in serialization (`serde`), web frameworks, and database ORMs.

Attribute-like Macros

Attribute-like macros allow developers to define new attributes. They are useful for marking functions, types, or modules and generating logic based on those markings.

Example:

```
#[route(GET, "/")]

fn index() {}
```

Creating it:

```
#[proc_macro_attribute]

pub fn route(attr: TokenStream, item: TokenStream) -> TokenStream {

    let meta = attr.to_string();

    let code = item.to_string();

    let output = format!("// route metadata: {}\n{}", meta, code);

    output.parse().unwrap()

}
```

Attribute-like macros are used extensively in Actix, Rocket, and other frameworks for declarative APIs.

Function-like Macros

These look like regular functions but are evaluated at compile time:

```
html! {

    <div>

        <h1>"Hello!"</h1>

    </div>
```

```
}
```

This macro turns custom markup into Rust code. The yew crate uses this pattern to emulate JSX.

To implement:

```
#[proc_macro]

pub fn html(input: TokenStream) -> TokenStream {

    // parse and generate HTML-like output

    unimplemented!()

}
```

Using syn and quote

The syn crate parses Rust code into an AST, and quote turns Rust code into token streams. This duo is the backbone of most procedural macros.

For example:

```
let ident = syn::parse_str::<syn::Ident>("MyType").unwrap();

let tokens = quote! {

    fn make() -> #ident {

        #ident {}

    }

};
```

This lets you manipulate identifiers, function definitions, type annotations, and more.

Real-World Use: Serde

Serde uses procedural macros to derive serialization and deserialization logic:

```
#[derive(Serialize, Deserialize)]
struct User {
    id: u32,
    name: String,
}
```

These macros inspect struct fields, generate boilerplate, and enforce correctness, all at compile time.

This model is more performant and safer than runtime reflection-based systems.

Metaprogramming with Build Scripts

Rust allows you to use `build.rs` to generate code at compile time based on external files, environment variables, or dynamic inputs.

Use case: Generating Rust constants from a config file.

Example `build.rs`:

```
use std::fs;

fn main() {
    let config = "pub const CONFIG_VERSION: &str = \"1.0.0\";";
    fs::write("src/generated.rs", config).unwrap();
}
```

In your main code:

```
include!("generated.rs");

fn main() {
    println!("Version: {}", CONFIG_VERSION);
}
```

This technique is used to embed resource files, generate bindings, or inject version numbers.

Combining Macros for DSLs

With procedural and declarative macros, you can build embedded domain-specific languages (DSLs). For example, consider a state machine:

```
state_machine! {
    Idle => [connect] => Connecting,
    Connecting => [success] => Active,
    Connecting => [fail] => Error
}
```

You can parse this structure and generate a Rust enum and a transition table.

Internally, this might generate:

```
enum State {
```

```
    Idle,

    Connecting,

    Active,

    Error,

}


impl State {

    fn transition(self, event: &str) -> Option<Self> {

        match (self, event) {

            (State::Idle, "connect") => Some(State::Connecting),

            (State::Connecting, "success") => Some(State::Active),

            (State::Connecting, "fail") => Some(State::Error),

            _ => None,

        }

    }

}
```

This approach gives you both expressiveness and correctness, backed by the compiler.

Safety and Limitations

Rust's metaprogramming is safe and hygienic by design. Unlike C macros, Rust macros don't suffer from accidental name collisions or undefined behavior.

Still, limitations include:

- Procedural macros can't access type information (no type inference).

- Compilation errors can be cryptic if not handled gracefully.

- Debugging macro-generated code requires `cargo expand`.

Hygiene also means macros can't easily access surrounding variables unless explicitly passed in.

Best Practices

- Use declarative macros for simple code repetition.

- Use procedural macros when inspecting structure or generating trait impls.

- Always document your macros clearly—macro code can be hard to read.

- Leverage `cargo expand` to understand what's generated.

- Keep macro-generated code readable and predictable.

- Validate inputs within macros; produce helpful compile-time errors.

Summary

Rust's metaprogramming capabilities give you the tools to write code that writes code—cleanly, safely, and efficiently. Whether you're reducing boilerplate with declarative macros, generating complex trait implementations with procedural macros, or embedding external data at compile time with build scripts, Rust empowers you to create expressive and maintainable abstractions.

Key tools and techniques:

- **Declarative macros** for patterns and repetition

- **Procedural macros** for structural introspection and expansion

- `syn` **and** `quote` for parsing and emitting code

- **Build scripts** for compile-time file and configuration processing

- **DSLs** and framework-level abstractions through custom macros

Rust's compile-time metaprogramming integrates seamlessly into the language's type system and safety model, enabling power without sacrificing clarity or correctness. By mastering these tools, you can write more expressive, maintainable, and DRY code—perfect for high-performance systems development.

Chapter 7: Systems Programming with Rust

Interfacing with C and FFI

Rust is a systems programming language, and one of the key responsibilities of any systems language is the ability to interact with other low-level languages, especially C. Since a vast amount of system software and libraries are written in C, the ability to call into C code (and be called from it) is crucial for interoperability. Rust handles this through its Foreign Function Interface (FFI), which allows seamless integration with external libraries while maintaining safety and performance.

This section will explore how Rust interfaces with C, how to call C code from Rust, how to expose Rust functions to C, and how to safely manage memory across this boundary.

Understanding the Basics of FFI

The FFI in Rust is centered around the `extern` keyword. It enables you to declare functions that are implemented in C and call them from Rust. Conversely, Rust functions can also be declared with `#[no_mangle] extern "C"` to make them accessible from C code.

The C calling convention is specified as `"C"` in Rust, which aligns with the standard ABI (Application Binary Interface) used by most C compilers. Rust provides the `libc` crate to offer bindings for C types and standard library functions, ensuring platform compatibility.

Calling C Code from Rust

Let's say you have a simple C library with the following function:

```
// mathlib.c

int add(int a, int b) {

    return a + b;

}
```

You can compile this C file into a static or shared library and then call the add function from Rust.

Step 1: Compile the C code

```
gcc -c mathlib.c -o mathlib.o

ar rcs libmathlib.a mathlib.o
```

Step 2: Declare the external function in Rust

```
extern "C" {

    fn add(a: i32, b: i32) -> i32;

}


fn main() {

    unsafe {

        let result = add(5, 7);

        println!("Result from C: {}", result);

    }

}
```

Step 3: Link the library

Update Cargo.toml to add build script support, then create a build.rs file:

```
[package]

build = "build.rs"
```

```rust
// build.rs

fn main() {

    println!("cargo:rustc-link-search=native=.");

    println!("cargo:rustc-link-lib=static=mathlib");

}
```

This setup tells Cargo where to find the static library and to link it during compilation.

Exposing Rust Functions to C

In some scenarios, you may want to write performance-critical code in Rust and call it from a C application. This is straightforward, but there are a few requirements to make it work.

1. Functions must use the C calling convention: `extern "C"`

2. Functions must not be name-mangled: use `#[no_mangle]`

3. Only C-compatible types should be used across the boundary

Here's a simple example:

```rust
// lib.rs


#[no_mangle]

pub extern "C" fn multiply(a: i32, b: i32) -> i32 {

    a * b

}
```

You can then build this Rust code as a shared library:

```
cargo build --release
```

This generates a `.so` or `.dll` file that can be linked and used from C.

C usage:

```c
#include <stdio.h>

extern int multiply(int a, int b);

int main() {
    int result = multiply(3, 4);
    printf("Result from Rust: %d\n", result);
    return 0;
}
```

Compile with:

```
gcc -o main main.c -L./target/release -lrustlib -ldl
```

C-Compatible Data Types

Rust and C have different representations for certain types. For example:

- `bool` in Rust is 1 byte (`true`/`false`), but in C it is typically an `int` (unless using `stdbool.h`)

- Structs and enums may have different memory layouts unless specifically marked

To bridge this gap, Rust offers the `#[repr(C)]` attribute. This forces Rust to use C-compatible memory layout and alignment rules.

```rust
#[repr(C)]

pub struct Point {

    x: f64,

    y: f64,

}
```

This struct can be safely shared between Rust and C, provided both sides agree on its layout.

Managing Memory Across FFI

Memory ownership and lifetime is one of the trickiest aspects of FFI. C code can't automatically understand or participate in Rust's ownership system, and vice versa. Therefore, you must establish clear rules:

- **Who allocates the memory?**

- **Who deallocates it?**

- **Is the memory layout agreed upon?**

For example, if Rust allocates a string, and C tries to free it using `free()`, you will get undefined behavior. To handle such scenarios:

1. Create allocation and deallocation functions in Rust.

2. Document clearly which side owns the memory.

```rust
use std::ffi::CString;

use std::os::raw::c_char;


#[no_mangle]

pub extern "C" fn get_greeting() -> *mut c_char {

    let greeting = CString::new("Hello from Rust!").unwrap();

    greeting.into_raw() // transfers ownership to C

}


#[no_mangle]

pub extern "C" fn free_string(s: *mut c_char) {

    if s.is_null() { return; }

    unsafe {

        CString::from_raw(s); // drops the CString, memory is freed

    }

}
```

C side:

```c
#include <stdio.h>

#include <stdlib.h>


extern char* get_greeting();

extern void free_string(char* s);
```

```
int main() {

    char* msg = get_greeting();

    printf("%s\n", msg);

    free_string(msg);

    return 0;

}
```

Using bindgen for Generating Rust Bindings

Manually writing Rust declarations for complex C headers can be error-prone. The bindgen tool automates this process by parsing C headers and generating Rust FFI bindings.

Install it:

```
cargo install bindgen
```

Generate bindings:

```
bindgen wrapper.h -o src/bindings.rs
```

You can then include the generated bindings in your Rust codebase.

Safety and unsafe Blocks

All FFI calls are inherently unsafe in Rust because Rust can't guarantee that the external code follows the same safety rules. Therefore, all calls to extern "C" functions must be wrapped in unsafe {} blocks.

This doesn't mean the code is broken—it means you, the developer, must uphold Rust's guarantees when calling into foreign code.

Key safety tips:

- Never trust external pointers without validating them

- Clearly document memory ownership expectations

- Avoid passing complex data structures unless memory layout is precisely known

- Test across platforms if portability is a goal

Building and Linking Strategies

There are several strategies for building and linking mixed C/Rust projects:

- **Static Linking:** Useful for embedding C code in Rust crates or vice versa. Easier to deploy.

- **Dynamic Linking:** Useful for shared libraries and plugin systems. Requires more care in deployment.

- **Inline C with cc crate:** For simple C code, you can embed and compile it as part of the Rust build using the cc crate.

Example: cc crate

```
[build-dependencies]

cc = "1.0"
```

```
// build.rs

fn main() {

    cc::Build::new()

        .file("src/mathlib.c")
```

```
        .compile("mathlib");

}
```

Real-World Applications

FFI in Rust is used extensively in production systems:

- **Operating systems** use FFI to interact with bootloaders and low-level system code.

- **Cryptography libraries** like `ring` use C code for low-level cryptographic primitives.

- **Game engines** integrate with graphics APIs like OpenGL and Vulkan through FFI.

- **Databases** embed Rust code in C applications for performance-critical workloads.

Many companies adopt Rust incrementally by first replacing C modules with Rust while maintaining the existing C architecture through FFI.

Summary

Rust's FFI capabilities make it a powerful tool for systems programming. Whether you're integrating with legacy C code, exposing safe Rust functions to C, or writing a full-blown OS kernel module, FFI gives you the tools to bridge the gap between modern safety and low-level control.

With great power comes great responsibility—FFI is inherently unsafe, and managing memory and contracts across language boundaries demands rigor. But when done carefully, Rust and C can coexist in a high-performance, maintainable codebase that brings together the best of both worlds.

Low-Level Memory Manipulation

Rust, unlike most modern languages, provides powerful low-level memory manipulation capabilities that are both performant and, when used carefully, safe. While the language encourages safe programming through its ownership model and strict type system, it also exposes a set of tools that allow direct control over memory layout, allocation, and mutation—comparable to C or C++.

This section explores how Rust enables low-level memory manipulation through raw pointers, manual allocation, unsafe blocks, unions, and direct interaction with memory-mapped I/O. These capabilities are essential for systems programming, embedded development, kernel modules, and performance-critical applications.

Raw Pointers: `*const T` and `*mut T`

Raw pointers in Rust are similar to those in C: they are non-owning, non-borrow-checked references that point to memory. These pointers can be `null`, dangling, or point to invalid memory, so any operation on them is `unsafe`.

```
fn main() {

    let x: i32 = 42;

    let r1 = &x as *const i32;

    let r2 = &x as *const i32;


    unsafe {

        println!("r1 points to: {}", *r1);

        println!("r2 points to: {}", *r2);

    }

}
```

Here, we convert a reference into a raw pointer and then dereference it within an `unsafe` block. This gives us fine-grained control over memory, bypassing the borrow checker.

You can also create mutable raw pointers using `*mut T`:

```
fn main() {

    let mut y = 10;

    let ptr = &mut y as *mut i32;
```

```
unsafe {

    *ptr += 1;

    println!("Updated value: {}", *ptr);

}

}
```

Raw pointers are essential when dealing with FFI, manually allocated memory, or when building abstractions like arenas or intrusive linked lists.

Manual Memory Allocation: `alloc` and `dealloc`

Rust's standard library provides low-level memory allocation APIs through the `std::alloc` module. This lets you allocate memory on the heap manually, without using collections like Vec or Box.

```
use std::alloc::{alloc, dealloc, Layout};

use std::ptr;


fn main() {

    unsafe {

        let layout = Layout::new::<u64>();

        let ptr = alloc(layout) as *mut u64;


        if !ptr.is_null() {

            *ptr = 1234;

            println!("Allocated value: {}", *ptr);
```

```
            dealloc(ptr as *mut u8, layout);

        }

    }

}
```

Here, we allocate enough space for a u64, store a value, and deallocate it manually. You must ensure the pointer is valid and not used after deallocation.

Manual allocation is particularly useful when building custom memory allocators, pools, or interacting with non-Rust APIs that require precise memory control.

Working with `MaybeUninit<T>`

The `std::mem::MaybeUninit<T>` type allows you to work with uninitialized memory safely. It is an essential building block when dealing with manual allocation or when you want to defer initialization.

```
use std::mem::MaybeUninit;


fn main() {

    let mut uninit: MaybeUninit<i32> = MaybeUninit::uninit();


    unsafe {

        uninit.as_mut_ptr().write(99);

        let value = uninit.assume_init();

        println!("Initialized: {}", value);

    }
```

222 | Rust Programming Mastery

```
}
```

This code avoids undefined behavior by writing to the memory before reading it. MaybeUninit is particularly useful for performance-sensitive code that needs to initialize arrays or buffers without default values.

Unsafe Unions

Unions in Rust allow overlapping memory regions for multiple data representations. This is useful when implementing tagged unions, bitfields, or FFI bindings to C unions.

```rust
union IntOrFloat {

    i: i32,

    f: f32,

}


fn main() {

    let mut value = IntOrFloat { i: 42 };


    unsafe {

        println!("As int: {}", value.i);

        value.f = 3.14;

        println!("As float: {}", value.f);

    }

}
```

Unions must be accessed inside unsafe blocks because they can easily cause undefined behavior if interpreted incorrectly. Rust unions do not have automatic drop logic—if they contain non-Copy types, you must manually manage destruction.

Memory Alignment and Padding

In low-level systems programming, memory alignment and structure padding are critical. Rust gives you full control using attributes like #[repr(C)], #[repr(align(N))], and #[repr(packed)].

```rust
#[repr(C)]

struct MyStruct {

    a: u8,

    b: u32,

}
```

In this example, the compiler may insert padding between a and b to ensure alignment. To inspect the layout, use:

```rust
use std::mem;


fn main() {

    println!("Size: {}", mem::size_of::<MyStruct>());

    println!("Align: {}", mem::align_of::<MyStruct>());

}
```

Packing a struct (with #[repr(packed)]) removes padding but can cause unaligned memory access, which is unsafe and can crash on some architectures.

Memory-Mapped I/O

Low-level hardware interactions often involve mapping device registers or memory into the address space of a program. Rust allows this with unsafe raw pointers.

Here's an example stub for memory-mapped I/O (note: only run in a real OS/dev env):

```
const MMIO_BASE: usize = 0x3F00_0000;
```

```
unsafe fn read_mmio(offset: usize) -> u32 {
    let ptr = (MMIO_BASE + offset) as *const u32;
    ptr.read_volatile()
}
```

```
unsafe fn write_mmio(offset: usize, value: u32) {
    let ptr = (MMIO_BASE + offset) as *mut u32;
    ptr.write_volatile(value);
}
```

`read_volatile` and `write_volatile` ensure the compiler does not optimize away memory accesses—critical for device communication.

Pointer Arithmetic and Casting

Rust permits pointer arithmetic within unsafe blocks:

```
fn main() {
    let arr = [1, 2, 3, 4, 5];
```

```
    let ptr = arr.as_ptr();


    unsafe {

        println!("{}", *ptr.add(2)); // prints 3

    }

}
```

You can also cast between pointer types:

```
let raw: *const u8 = &10u32 as *const u32 as *const u8;
```

Pointer casting must be done carefully to avoid aliasing and alignment issues. You must uphold alignment guarantees manually.

Simulating `malloc` and `free`

To simulate a manual heap model, you can use the allocator APIs as a basic replacement for `malloc`/`free`:

```
use std::alloc::{alloc_zeroed, Layout};


fn main() {

    unsafe {

        let layout = Layout::array::<u32>(10).unwrap();

        let ptr = alloc_zeroed(layout) as *mut u32;


        for i in 0..10 {
```

```
        *ptr.add(i) = i as u32;

    }


    for i in 0..10 {

        println!("{}", *ptr.add(i));

    }


    std::alloc::dealloc(ptr as *mut u8, layout);

    }

}
```

This zero-initializes a buffer for 10 u32 values, then manually populates and deallocates it.

Building a Custom Allocator

Advanced systems may need custom memory allocation strategies, e.g., for embedded systems or real-time applications. You can define your own allocator by implementing the GlobalAlloc trait.

```
use std::alloc::{GlobalAlloc, Layout, System};


struct MyAllocator;


unsafe impl GlobalAlloc for MyAllocator {

    unsafe fn alloc(&self, layout: Layout) -> *mut u8 {

        println!("Allocating: {}", layout.size());
```

```
        System.alloc(layout)

    }


    unsafe fn dealloc(&self, ptr: *mut u8, layout: Layout) {

        println!("Deallocating: {}", layout.size());

        System.dealloc(ptr, layout)

    }

}


#[global_allocator]

static GLOBAL: MyAllocator = MyAllocator;
```

This logs allocation events while delegating actual work to the system allocator. You can replace it with any strategy (slab, arena, etc.).

Inline Assembly and Intrinsics

For the lowest level of control, Rust supports inline assembly (asm!) via core::arch. This allows you to write architecture-specific instructions, like CPU hints or hardware operations.

Example (x86_64):

```
use std::arch::asm;


fn main() {

    unsafe {

        asm!("nop");

    }
```

```
}
```

Be warned: inline assembly is architecture-specific, hard to test, and should only be used when no higher abstraction suffices.

Summary

Rust's low-level memory manipulation tools rival those of C and C++, offering unmatched control with a modern type system and explicit safety boundaries. With raw pointers, manual allocation, uninitialized memory handling, and memory layout control, Rust enables system-level tasks from OS kernels to memory-mapped I/O to high-performance libraries.

However, the power comes with the responsibility to uphold memory safety manually when stepping outside the compiler's protection. That means disciplined use of unsafe, rigorous documentation, and defensive coding practices. Mastery of these tools makes Rust not only safe for the average case but powerful enough for the hardest problems in systems programming.

Writing Efficient and Safe Embedded Code

Embedded systems development presents a unique set of challenges: limited memory, real-time constraints, lack of operating systems, and direct hardware interaction. Rust is increasingly becoming a go-to language for this domain due to its emphasis on safety, zero-cost abstractions, and precise control over memory and concurrency.

In this section, we explore how Rust enables embedded systems programming. We will walk through the key principles of writing safe and efficient embedded code in Rust, understand the toolchain, manage resources manually, and interact directly with hardware. You'll learn how to use crates like embedded-hal, cortex-m, and no_std to build real-world applications that run on bare metal.

The no_std Environment

Rust's standard library is not suitable for most embedded environments due to its reliance on OS-level features like threads, heap allocation, or file I/O. For these scenarios, Rust supports a subset of the language that omits the standard library, known as no_std.

```
#![no_std]
```

```
fn main() {

    // This won't work; `main` is not used in most bare-metal
applications.

}
```

Instead of using `std`, you use `core`, which provides essential components like:

- `Option`, `Result`

- Iterators

- Math utilities

- `Clone`, `Copy`, `PartialEq`, etc.

To enable `no_std`, simply add `#![no_std]` at the crate root. Most embedded projects use `#![no_main]` as well, since there's no operating system to invoke a `main` function.

Bare-Metal Rust with `cortex-m-rt`

For ARM Cortex-M based microcontrollers, the `cortex-m-rt` crate provides runtime support. Here's a minimal setup using `cortex-m`, `cortex-m-rt`, and a device-specific crate like `stm32f4`.

```
[dependencies]

cortex-m = "0.7"

cortex-m-rt = "0.7"

panic-halt = "0.2"


[dependencies.stm32f4]

version = "0.14"
```

```
features = ["stm32f401", "rt"]
```

Rust embedded uses device crates generated by svd2rust, which provide access to memory-mapped registers and peripherals using safe abstractions.

Example main.rs:

```rust
#![no_main]
#![no_std]


use cortex_m_rt::entry;
use panic_halt as _;


#[entry]
fn main() -> ! {
    loop {
        // your embedded logic here
    }
}
```

The #[entry] macro defines the entry point instead of main, and panic_halt stops execution on panic without requiring OS support.

Accessing Hardware Peripherals

Rust embedded projects often use the Peripheral Access Crate (PAC) and Hardware Abstraction Layer (HAL) for your target device. PACs provide low-level access, while HALs offer a safer, more abstract interface.

Example with an STM32 microcontroller:

```
let peripherals = stm32f4::stm32f401::Peripherals::take().unwrap();

let gpioa = peripherals.GPIOA.split();

let pa5 = gpioa.pa5.into_push_pull_output();
```

This safely enables GPIO pin A5 as an output pin.

You don't have to worry about pointer dereferencing or register bitmasks—everything is generated from the chip's SVD file and is checked by the compiler.

Embedded HAL and Drivers

The embedded-hal crate defines a set of traits for generic embedded hardware—such as GPIOs, I2C, SPI, and timers—that HALs can implement.

```
use embedded_hal::digital::v2::OutputPin;
```

```
let mut led = ...; // from your HAL

led.set_high().unwrap();
```

This abstraction allows you to write platform-independent code. You can develop libraries and drivers that work on any microcontroller that implements embedded-hal.

Memory Safety and Concurrency

Rust's ownership model shines in embedded systems by preventing data races and use-after-free bugs at compile time. In a no_std environment, where you lack dynamic allocation and OS-based scheduling, this matters even more.

Example: toggling an LED from two contexts (main and interrupt):

```rust
static mut LED: Option<Pin<Output<PushPull>>> = None;


#[entry]

fn main() -> ! {

    let gpioa = ...;

    let led = gpioa.pa5.into_push_pull_output();


    unsafe {

        LED = Some(led);

    }


    // Enable interrupt...

}


#[interrupt]

fn TIM2() {

    unsafe {

        if let Some(ref mut led) = LED {

            led.toggle().unwrap();

        }

    }

}
```

This is inherently unsafe, and better solutions involve using the `cortex-m`'s critical section API or `RTIC` (Real-Time Interrupt-driven Concurrency) framework for safe concurrent access.

Real-Time Interrupt-driven Concurrency (RTIC)

RTIC is a lightweight real-time framework for embedded Rust. It replaces the traditional `main` + `interrupt` pattern with task definitions that enforce safe shared resource access at compile time.

```rust
#[rtic::app(device = stm32f4::stm32f401)]

mod app {

    #[resources]

    struct Resources {

        led: gpio::Pin<Output<PushPull>>,

    }


    #[init]

    fn init(cx: init::Context) -> init::LateResources {

        // Setup hardware...

        init::LateResources {

            led: gpio_pin,

        }

    }


    #[task(binds = TIM2, resources = [led])]

    fn tim2(cx: tim2::Context) {
```

```
        cx.resources.led.toggle().unwrap();

    }

}
```

RTIC ensures that `led` can't be accessed concurrently between tasks without appropriate locking or prioritization. This makes embedded concurrency safe and deterministic.

Panic Handling and Logging

Embedded systems can't use `println!`, so error handling is tricky. You must use a panic handler that fits your environment.

`panic-halt` just stops execution. `panic-itm`, `panic-semihosting`, or `rtt-target` can send logs to your debugger or development console.

Example with RTT logging:

```
use rtt_target::{rprintln, rtt_init_print};


#[entry]

fn main() -> ! {

    rtt_init_print!();

    rprintln!("System initialized");


    loop {}

}
```

RTT is fast and non-blocking, ideal for real-time logging without UART overhead.

Efficient Code: Inline, Zero-Cost, Const

Rust's zero-cost abstraction principle means high-level constructs are optimized away when not used. You can explicitly request inlining or mark constants at compile time.

```
#[inline(always)]

fn fast_add(a: u32, b: u32) -> u32 {

    a + b

}



const FREQ: u32 = 48_000_000;
```

You can also use `const fn` to perform computations at compile time, reducing runtime overhead.

Working Without the Heap

In embedded, heap allocation is often disabled or discouraged. You must rely on stack allocation, static memory, or fixed-size buffers.

```
static mut BUFFER: [u8; 256] = [0; 256];
```

This static buffer is accessible from any function or interrupt handler with `unsafe`. Alternatives include crates like `heapless`, which offer stack-allocated data structures.

```
use heapless::Vec;


let mut v: Vec<u8, 8> = Vec::new();

v.push(1).unwrap();
```

This gives you a `Vec`-like structure with no heap use and compile-time bounds.

Bootloaders, Startup, and Linker Scripts

Bare-metal applications require full control over startup code, memory layout, and reset behavior. The `cortex-m-rt` crate generates startup code and linker scripts by default, but you can customize it.

Memory layout is controlled via `memory.x`:

```
MEMORY

{

  FLASH : ORIGIN = 0x08000000, LENGTH = 512K

  RAM   : ORIGIN = 0x20000000, LENGTH = 128K

}
```

You can define the stack, heap, and section placement manually if needed.

Device Abstraction with `embedded-hal` Traits

Instead of writing one-off code for a sensor, use traits:

```
pub struct TemperatureSensor<I2C> {

    i2c: I2C,

    address: u8,

}



impl<I2C, E> TemperatureSensor<I2C>
```

```
where

    I2C: embedded_hal::blocking::i2c::WriteRead<Error = E>,

{

    pub fn read_temp(&mut self) -> Result<u16, E> {

        let mut buf = [0; 2];

        self.i2c.write_read(self.address, &[0x01], &mut buf)?;

        Ok(u16::from_be_bytes(buf))

    }

}
```

This makes your code portable across chips, testable on desktop, and decoupled from hardware details.

Summary

Rust transforms embedded development by combining zero-cost abstractions with compile-time safety. You get memory safety, concurrency without fear, hardware access without undefined behavior, and compile-time guarantees—all critical in a domain where every byte and cycle matters.

Through the use of `no_std`, HALs, PACs, RTIC, and efficient design principles, you can write embedded software that is not only correct but also portable, efficient, and maintainable.

The ecosystem is still growing, but what exists today is already robust enough to build production-ready systems—from sensor controllers to drones, medical devices, and bare-metal OS kernels. Rust brings modern safety to the most unforgiving environments.

Building Custom OS Kernels and Drivers

Rust's increasing presence in systems-level development has opened doors for safe and efficient OS development. Traditionally, operating system kernels and drivers have been the domain of C and assembly, but Rust brings powerful tools like zero-cost abstractions, strong typing, and memory safety—even in the absence of a standard library or runtime. In this section, we will explore how to build a custom OS kernel in Rust from the ground up and how to implement drivers in this environment.

We'll cover bootloader interaction, the `no_std` and `no_main` environment, memory layout, interrupts, and device driver architecture. By the end, you'll understand how to construct a minimal yet functional OS kernel and add custom drivers to interact with real hardware.

Kernel Development Fundamentals in Rust

Unlike user-space programs, kernels do not have access to an operating system—they *are* the operating system. This means no heap allocation (unless you implement it), no standard library, and no main function in the traditional sense.

To get started, we must configure our environment to:

- Disable the standard library

- Define a custom entry point

- Provide our own panic handler

- Use a bootloader to transition into our code

Let's build a basic x86_64 kernel.

Initial Project Setup

First, we create a new binary crate:

```
cargo new rustos --bin

cd rustos
```

Edit `Cargo.toml`:

```
[package]

name = "rustos"

version = "0.1.0"
```

```
edition = "2021"


[dependencies]

bootloader = "0.11.2"


[build-dependencies]

bootimage = "0.10.2"


[package.metadata.bootimage]

default-target = "x86_64-rustos.json"
```

And configure it for no standard library:

```
#![no_std]

#![no_main]
```

Custom Target Specification

Since we're not targeting Linux or Windows, we must define a custom target. Create
x86_64-rustos.json:

```
{

    "llvm-target": "x86_64-unknown-none",

    "data-layout": "e-m:e-i64:64-f80:128-n8:16:32:64-S128",

    "arch": "x86_64",
```

```
  "os": "none",

  "executables": true,

  "linker-flavor": "ld.lld",

  "linker": "rust-lld",

  "panic-strategy": "abort",

  "disable-redzone": true,

  "features": "-mmx,-sse,+soft-float"

}
```

This tells Rust to emit bare-metal x86_64 code with no assumptions about the OS.

Entry Point and Bootloader

Use the `bootloader` crate to load your kernel. This provides a simple 64-bit ELF loader with framebuffer and memory map support.

Set up your `main.rs`:

```rust
#![no_std]

#![no_main]


use core::panic::PanicInfo;


#[no_mangle]

pub extern "C" fn _start() -> ! {

    loop {}

}
```

```
#[panic_handler]

fn panic(_info: &PanicInfo) -> ! {

    loop {}

}
```

Here, _start is the entry point—executed directly after the bootloader passes control to your kernel.

Build it with bootimage:

```
cargo install bootimage

cargo bootimage
```

You'll get a .bin image that can be booted via QEMU:

```
qemu-system-x86_64 -drive format=raw,file=target/x86_64-
rustos/debug/bootimage-rustos.bin
```

VGA Output: Writing to the Screen

Let's display text by writing directly to VGA memory, which begins at 0xb8000.

```
const VGA_BUFFER: *mut u8 = 0xb8000 as *mut u8;


#[no_mangle]

pub extern "C" fn _start() -> ! {
```

```
    let hello = b"Hello Kernel!";

    for (i, &byte) in hello.iter().enumerate() {

        unsafe {

            *VGA_BUFFER.offset(i as isize * 2) = byte;

            *VGA_BUFFER.offset(i as isize * 2 + 1) = 0x0f; // white
on black

        }

    }


    loop {}

}
```

We write characters and attributes (color) directly to video memory. This gives immediate visual confirmation that our kernel is running.

Paging and Memory Management

A real kernel must manage memory. Rust makes this safe and powerful with the help of x86_64, a crate that provides abstractions over the x86_64 architecture, including paging.

Add dependencies:

```
[dependencies]

x86_64 = "0.14.9"
```

Example: reading the current page table base:

```
use x86_64::registers::control::Cr3;
```

```
let (frame, _) = Cr3::read();
```

You can then walk the page table hierarchy and map virtual memory to physical frames. Implementing a full frame allocator requires parsing the memory map provided by the bootloader and allocating physical frames safely.

Interrupts and Exceptions

Hardware interrupts and CPU exceptions must be handled explicitly. Rust offers facilities via the x86-interrupt calling convention.

```
use x86_64::structures::idt::{InterruptDescriptorTable,
InterruptStackFrame};
```

```
static mut IDT: InterruptDescriptorTable =
InterruptDescriptorTable::new();
```

```
pub fn init_idt() {

    unsafe {

        IDT.breakpoint.set_handler_fn(breakpoint_handler);

        IDT.load();

    }

}
```

```
extern "x86-interrupt" fn breakpoint_handler(stack_frame:
InterruptStackFrame) {

    println!("EXCEPTION: BREAKPOINT\n{:#?}", stack_frame);
```

```
}
```

You must ensure that handler functions follow ABI expectations and are safely defined.

You can also define handlers for hardware IRQs (e.g., keyboard, timer) and link them with the PIC (Programmable Interrupt Controller) using crates like pic8259.

Writing a Driver: Example - PS/2 Keyboard

A typical PS/2 keyboard maps its data port to 0x60. To read a scancode, we can do:

```rust
pub fn read_scancode() -> u8 {

    unsafe {

        let port = 0x60 as *const u8;

        port.read_volatile()

    }

}
```

You'll typically set up a hardware IRQ handler for interrupt 33 (IRQ1) and invoke this function.

A basic driver might look like this:

```rust
use pc_keyboard::{layouts, HandleControl, Keyboard, ScancodeSet1};

use spin::Mutex;


lazy_static! {

    static ref KEYBOARD: Mutex<Keyboard<layouts::Us104Key,
ScancodeSet1>> =
```

```
    Mutex::new(Keyboard::new(layouts::Us104Key, ScancodeSet1,
HandleControl::Ignore));

}


extern "x86-interrupt" fn keyboard_interrupt_handler(_stack:
InterruptStackFrame) {

    let scancode = read_scancode();

    let mut keyboard = KEYBOARD.lock();


    if let Ok(Some(key_event)) = keyboard.add_byte(scancode) {

        if let Some(key) = keyboard.process_keyevent(key_event) {

            print!("{}", key);

        }

    }


    // Acknowledge interrupt

    unsafe {
pic8259::PICS.lock().notify_end_of_interrupt(InterruptIndex::Keyboar
d.as_u8()) };

}
```

This provides a fully operational keyboard input system at a low level.

Writing a Device Driver Framework

To scale drivers, abstract the concept of a device:

```rust
pub trait Device {

    fn name(&self) -> &str;

    fn init(&mut self);

    fn read(&self) -> Option<u8>;

    fn write(&mut self, data: u8);

}
```

Each device can implement its specific logic behind this trait. This allows the kernel to maintain a registry of devices and access them generically.

File System and Storage Driver

Drivers for block devices like ATA disks or SD cards use I/O ports or MMIO.

For example, ATA uses I/O ports like 0x1F0 for data and 0x1F7 for status.

```rust
unsafe fn ata_read_sector(lba: u32, buffer: &mut [u16; 256]) {

    let port_data = 0x1F0 as *mut u16;


    // Setup LBA

    outb(0x1F6, 0xE0 | ((lba >> 24) & 0x0F) as u8);

    outb(0x1F2, 1);

    outb(0x1F3, lba as u8);

    outb(0x1F4, (lba >> 8) as u8);

    outb(0x1F5, (lba >> 16) as u8);

    outb(0x1F7, 0x20);
```

```rust
// Wait for data ready, then read 256 words

for i in 0..256 {

    buffer[i] = port_data.read_volatile();

}

}
```

This is foundational for writing file systems or virtual memory backings.

Multitasking and Context Switching

To implement a multitasking OS, you'll need to switch contexts between processes or threads. This involves:

- Saving/restoring registers

- Managing stacks and paging

- Scheduling logic (e.g., round-robin or priority-based)

Rust allows you to write context switchers in inline assembly or using external crates. You'll also need to handle privilege level transitions via rings (user/kernel mode), using hardware features like the Task State Segment (TSS).

Summary

Building a custom OS kernel and drivers in Rust requires deep knowledge of low-level systems, but the language provides invaluable tools:

- `no_std`, `no_main`, and custom entry points for bare-metal environments

- Direct memory and I/O port access with memory safety

- Interrupt handling and concurrency with correctness guarantees

- Abstract drivers and device management via traits

- Efficient memory and task management without runtime cost

Rust empowers kernel developers with a modern, safe, and powerful language while retaining the low-level access traditionally reserved for C and assembly. As the community and ecosystem grow, it's increasingly feasible to write production-level OS kernels, drivers, and bootloaders entirely in Rust.

Chapter 8: Rust for Web and Network Programming

Web Frameworks: Actix and Rocket

Rust has quickly risen in popularity not only for systems-level programming but also for building highly performant, scalable web applications. Its powerful type system, memory safety guarantees, and asynchronous programming model make it an attractive option for backend development. In this section, we'll explore two of the most prominent web frameworks in the Rust ecosystem: Actix Web and Rocket. Each framework takes a different approach to building web applications but both share Rust's core values of performance and safety.

Introducing Actix Web

Actix Web is one of the most performant web frameworks available in the Rust ecosystem. It is built on top of the Actix actor framework, which enables highly concurrent and scalable applications. Actix Web is asynchronous by design and uses the Tokio runtime under the hood.

To get started with Actix Web, add the following dependencies to your `Cargo.toml`:

```
[dependencies]

actix-web = "4"

tokio = { version = "1", features = ["full"] }
```

A Basic Actix Web Server

Here is a simple Actix Web server that responds to a GET request at the root path:

```
use actix_web::{get, App, HttpServer, Responder};


#[get("/")]
```

```rust
async fn hello() -> impl Responder {

    "Hello from Actix Web!"

}


#[tokio::main]

async fn main() -> std::io::Result<()> {

    HttpServer::new(|| {

        App::new()

            .service(hello)

    })

    .bind("127.0.0.1:8080")?

    .run()

    .await

}
```

This example demonstrates the basic structure of an Actix Web application. The App acts as the main application container, where you register routes and middleware. Each route can be an async function, making it easy to handle I/O-bound operations.

Routing and Request Handling in Actix

Actix Web supports RESTful routing out of the box. You can define handlers for different HTTP methods and paths using macros like #[get], #[post], etc.

```rust
use actix_web::{post, web, HttpResponse};


#[post("/submit")]
```

```
async fn submit(data: web::Json<MyData>) -> HttpResponse {

    HttpResponse::Ok().body(format!("Received: {:?}", data))

}
```

```
#[derive(serde::Deserialize, Debug)]

struct MyData {

    name: String,

    age: u32,

}
```

This snippet shows how to handle POST requests with JSON payloads. Actix Web integrates seamlessly with the serde crate for deserialization.

Middleware and Error Handling in Actix

Middleware is used to intercept requests and responses for logging, authentication, and more. Actix Web provides a middleware API that lets you add custom logic at various stages.

Example of a simple logging middleware:

```
use actix_web::{dev::ServiceRequest, middleware::Logger, App,
HttpServer};
```

```
HttpServer::new(|| {

    App::new()

        .wrap(Logger::default())

        .service(hello)

})
```

Error handling can be done using custom types and `Result`. You can define your own error types and implement the `ResponseError` trait.

Introducing Rocket

Rocket is another popular web framework for Rust, focusing on developer ergonomics and a high-level abstraction over request handling. It uses Rust's macro system extensively to reduce boilerplate, making it intuitive to define routes and extract parameters.

To start with Rocket, add it to your `Cargo.toml`:

```toml
[dependencies]
rocket = { version = "0.5.0-rc.2", features = ["json"] }
```

Rocket requires a nightly Rust compiler due to its reliance on unstable features, but offers a clean and expressive API.

A Basic Rocket Application

```rust
#[macro_use] extern crate rocket;

#[get("/")]
fn index() -> &'static str {
    "Hello from Rocket!"
}

#[launch]
fn rocket() -> _ {
    rocket::build().mount("/", routes![index])
```

```
}
```

This application mounts a single GET route at the root. Rocket automatically infers route parameters and return types, reducing the need for boilerplate code.

Routing and Data Extraction in Rocket

Rocket supports route parameters, query strings, and form data out of the box.

```
#[get("/user/<id>")]

fn user(id: i32) -> String {

    format!("User ID: {}", id)

}
```

For JSON payloads, Rocket uses the serde crate for deserialization:

```
use rocket::serde::{json::Json, Deserialize};


#[derive(Deserialize)]

struct Info {

    name: String,

    age: u8,

}


#[post("/info", format = "json", data = "<info>")]

fn info(info: Json<Info>) -> String {
```

```
    format!("Name: {}, Age: {}", info.name, info.age)

}
```

Rocket Fairings and Error Catching

Fairings in Rocket are similar to middleware in Actix. They allow you to hook into the application lifecycle for tasks like logging, compression, or modifying requests/responses.

Error handling in Rocket can be done using catchers:

```
#[catch(404)]

fn not_found() -> &'static str {

    "Resource not found"

}


rocket::build()

    .mount("/", routes![index])

    .register("/", catchers![not_found])
```

This code registers a custom handler for 404 errors, improving user experience and debugging.

Choosing Between Actix and Rocket

Both Actix and Rocket are capable web frameworks, and the choice between them often comes down to specific needs:

Feature	Actix Web	Rocket

Performance	High	Moderate to High
Developer Ergonomics	Moderate	Very High
Asynchronous	Yes (Tokio)	Planned/Partial
Stability	Stable	Uses nightly Rust (as of v0.5)
Ecosystem	Mature	Growing

Actix is suitable for applications that require maximum performance and concurrency, whereas Rocket is ideal for rapid development with a cleaner syntax and less boilerplate.

Full REST API Example with Actix

Let's build a simple REST API using Actix Web that allows us to perform CRUD operations on a list of users.

```rust
use actix_web::{web, App, HttpResponse, HttpServer, Responder};

use serde::{Deserialize, Serialize};

use std::sync::Mutex;


#[derive(Serialize, Deserialize)]

struct User {

    id: usize,

    name: String,

}
```

```rust
struct AppState {

    users: Mutex<Vec<User>>,

}


async fn get_users(data: web::Data<AppState>) -> impl Responder {

    let users = data.users.lock().unwrap();

    HttpResponse::Ok().json(&*users)

}


async fn add_user(user: web::Json<User>, data: web::Data<AppState>)
-> impl Responder {

    let mut users = data.users.lock().unwrap();

    users.push(user.into_inner());

    HttpResponse::Created().finish()

}


#[actix_web::main]

async fn main() -> std::io::Result<()> {

    let data = web::Data::new(AppState {

        users: Mutex::new(vec![]),

    });


    HttpServer::new(move || {

        App::new()

            .app_data(data.clone())
```

```
            .route("/users", web::get().to(get_users))

            .route("/users", web::post().to(add_user))

    })

    .bind("127.0.0.1:8080")?

    .run()

    .await

}
```

This API includes an in-memory store protected by a mutex. While not suitable for production, it's great for learning and prototyping. It demonstrates async handlers, shared state, and JSON serialization.

Conclusion

Both Actix Web and Rocket are robust frameworks with their own strengths. Actix shines in performance and scalability, while Rocket provides a more pleasant developer experience. Understanding how to use both gives you the flexibility to choose the right tool for the job.

In the next section, we'll dive deeper into asynchronous networking using Tokio and how to build real-time, non-blocking applications in Rust. With this foundation in web frameworks, you're now equipped to start building full-fledged web apps in Rust.

Networking with Tokio and Async Rust

Networking is one of the most powerful applications of asynchronous programming, and Rust, with its `async`/`await` syntax and the Tokio runtime, provides a high-performance foundation for building modern network applications. Tokio is the de facto asynchronous runtime for Rust and powers a vast ecosystem of crates and services, from microservices to real-time communication platforms.

In this section, we'll cover the fundamentals of networking with Tokio, including TCP and UDP communication, managing concurrent tasks, handling errors, and building real-world asynchronous servers and clients.

Why Async Networking?

Traditional synchronous networking involves blocking operations: when a socket is waiting for data, the entire thread halts until data arrives. This model is simple, but it doesn't scale well, especially when dealing with thousands of connections.

Async networking allows the program to perform other tasks while waiting for network I/O, improving throughput and responsiveness. Tokio enables this model in Rust by providing:

- A multi-threaded asynchronous runtime

- Non-blocking TCP/UDP sockets

- Timers, channels, and utilities for async workflows

- Integration with `futures` and `async/await`

Setting Up Tokio

To use Tokio, add the following to your `Cargo.toml`:

```toml
[dependencies]

tokio = { version = "1", features = ["full"] }
```

The `"full"` feature includes all the most commonly used components like I/O, TCP, UDP, time, macros, and more.

Writing an Async TCP Echo Server

Let's begin with a basic TCP server that accepts connections and echoes back anything it receives:

```rust
use tokio::net::TcpListener;

use tokio::io::{AsyncReadExt, AsyncWriteExt};


#[tokio::main]
```

```rust
async fn main() -> std::io::Result<()> {

    let listener = TcpListener::bind("127.0.0.1:8080").await?;

    println!("Listening on 127.0.0.1:8080");


    loop {

        let (mut socket, addr) = listener.accept().await?;

        println!("Accepted connection from {}", addr);


        tokio::spawn(async move {

            let mut buf = [0; 1024];


            loop {

                let n = match socket.read(&mut buf).await {

                    Ok(0) => return,

                    Ok(n) => n,

                    Err(e) => {

                            eprintln!("failed to read from socket; err =
{:?}", e);

                            return;

                    }

                };


                if let Err(e) = socket.write_all(&buf[0..n]).await {

                        eprintln!("failed to write to socket; err =
{:?}", e);
```

```
                    return;

            }

        }

    });

  }

}
```

This echo server listens for connections, reads data asynchronously, and writes it back to the client. The use of `tokio::spawn` allows each connection to be handled concurrently without blocking the main listener loop.

Understanding Async Tasks

`tokio::spawn` creates a lightweight green thread (task) that runs independently. Unlike OS threads, tasks are cheap and allow thousands of concurrent operations.

You can use `.await` inside any async context, and multiple tasks can be managed concurrently using `tokio::join!`, `tokio::select!`, or channels.

Creating an Async TCP Client

Let's build a TCP client that connects to our echo server, sends a message, and prints the response:

```rust
use tokio::net::TcpStream;

use tokio::io::{AsyncWriteExt, AsyncReadExt};


#[tokio::main]

async fn main() -> std::io::Result<()> {

    let mut stream = TcpStream::connect("127.0.0.1:8080").await?;
```

```
    stream.write_all(b"Hello, server!").await?;


    let mut buf = vec![0; 1024];

    let n = stream.read(&mut buf).await?;

    println!("Received: {}", String::from_utf8_lossy(&buf[..n]));


    Ok(())

}
```

UDP Communication in Tokio

UDP is connectionless and suitable for scenarios where performance is more important than guaranteed delivery (e.g., real-time games, video streaming). Here's a simple UDP echo server:

```
use tokio::net::UdpSocket;


#[tokio::main]
async fn main() -> std::io::Result<()> {

    let socket = UdpSocket::bind("127.0.0.1:8081").await?;

    let mut buf = [0u8; 1024];


    loop {

        let (len, addr) = socket.recv_from(&mut buf).await?;

        socket.send_to(&buf[..len], &addr).await?;

    }
```

```
}
```

And a client to test it:

```
use tokio::net::UdpSocket;


#[tokio::main]
async fn main() -> std::io::Result<()> {
    let socket = UdpSocket::bind("0.0.0.0:0").await?;
    socket.connect("127.0.0.1:8081").await?;


    socket.send(b"Hello UDP!").await?;
    let mut buf = [0; 1024];
    let n = socket.recv(&mut buf).await?;


    println!("Received: {}", String::from_utf8_lossy(&buf[..n]));
    Ok(())
}
```

Timeouts and Delays

Networking often requires managing timeouts and retry logic. Tokio provides powerful primitives for these scenarios:

```
use tokio::time::{timeout, Duration};
```

```
async fn do_network_call() -> Result<(), &'static str> {

    // Simulate long-running operation

    tokio::time::sleep(Duration::from_secs(3)).await;

    Ok(())

}


#[tokio::main]

async fn main() {

    match timeout(Duration::from_secs(2), do_network_call()).await {

        Ok(res) => println!("Operation finished: {:?}", res),

        Err(_) => println!("Operation timed out"),

    }

}
```

The `timeout` function wraps any future and returns an error if it doesn't complete in the specified duration.

Managing Connections with Channels

In a real-world application, you may want to coordinate between tasks using channels. Tokio provides `mpsc` and `broadcast` channels for message passing.

```
use tokio::sync::mpsc;


#[tokio::main]
```

```rust
async fn main() {

    let (tx, mut rx) = mpsc::channel(32);


    tokio::spawn(async move {

        tx.send("Hello from task").await.unwrap();

    });


    while let Some(message) = rx.recv().await {

        println!("Received: {}", message);

    }

}
```

Graceful Shutdown

A network server must handle termination gracefully, cleaning up connections and resources. One common approach is using a signal handler:

```rust
use tokio::signal;


#[tokio::main]

async fn main() {

    tokio::select! {

        _ = run_server() => {},

        _ = signal::ctrl_c() => {

            println!("Shutting down gracefully...");
```

```
        },

    }

}


async fn run_server() {

    // Your server logic here

}
```

This pattern ensures that the server can be interrupted (e.g., Ctrl+C) and still perform cleanup.

A Real-World Example: Chat Server

Let's build a simplified chat server using TCP and broadcast channels.

```
use tokio::{

    net::TcpListener,

    io::{AsyncBufReadExt, AsyncWriteExt, BufReader},

    sync::broadcast,

};


#[tokio::main]

async fn main() -> std::io::Result<()> {

    let listener = TcpListener::bind("127.0.0.1:8082").await?;

    let (tx, _) = broadcast::channel(100);
```

```
loop {

    let (socket, _) = listener.accept().await?;

    let tx = tx.clone();

    let mut rx = tx.subscribe();


    tokio::spawn(async move {

        let (reader, mut writer) = socket.into_split();

        let mut reader = BufReader::new(reader).lines();


        tokio::spawn(async move {

            while let Ok(msg) = rx.recv().await {

                writer.write_all(msg.as_bytes()).await.unwrap();

                writer.write_all(b"\n").await.unwrap();

            }

        });


        while let Ok(Some(line)) = reader.next_line().await {

            if tx.send(line).is_err() {

                break;

            }

        }

    });

}

}
```

This server accepts multiple TCP clients, broadcasts received messages to all clients using a `broadcast` channel, and allows real-time communication between them.

Error Handling Best Practices

Proper error handling in async applications is crucial. You should:

- Use `Result<T, E>` types consistently.

- Match all potential error cases using `match` or ?.

- Use structured logging (e.g., `tracing` crate) in production for better visibility.

Example:

```
use thiserror::Error;


#[derive(Error, Debug)]

enum MyError {

    #[error("I/O Error")]

    Io(#[from] std::io::Error),


    #[error("Invalid Input")]

    InvalidInput,

}
```

Custom error types help encapsulate error logic and make APIs more expressive.

Performance Considerations

When building async network applications, keep in mind:

- Avoid blocking the async runtime. Use `tokio::task::spawn_blocking` for CPU-bound work.

- Reuse connections when possible.

- Use structured logging to trace performance bottlenecks.

- Monitor with tools like `tokio-console` for runtime metrics.

Conclusion

Tokio and async Rust make it possible to write highly performant, concurrent network applications in a safe and scalable manner. From basic echo servers to complex chat applications, the abstractions provided by Tokio offer both low-level control and ergonomic APIs.

As you build more advanced systems, consider layering features like TLS (with `tokio-rustls`), HTTP (with `hyper` or `reqwest`), or even message queues (with `nats.rs` or `lapin`).

In the next section, we'll explore how to build RESTful APIs and microservices using Rust's web frameworks with async capabilities, putting your networking knowledge into practice.

Building REST APIs and Microservices

Modern web applications and distributed systems increasingly rely on REST APIs and microservice architectures to deliver scalable, modular, and maintainable solutions. Rust, with its focus on safety, performance, and modern concurrency, is particularly well-suited for building robust web backends. In this section, we will explore how to create fully functional REST APIs in Rust, structure microservices, and incorporate key features such as routing, validation, authentication, and inter-service communication.

We will primarily use **Actix Web** for the examples, as it offers excellent performance, mature ecosystem support, and full async compatibility via Tokio. By the end of this section, you'll understand the fundamental components of a RESTful Rust service and how to build and organize a real-world microservice architecture.

Fundamentals of a REST API

A REST API (Representational State Transfer) is a stateless client-server architecture that uses standard HTTP methods for interaction:

- GET – Retrieve resources

- POST – Create new resources

- PUT/PATCH – Update existing resources

- DELETE – Remove resources

In Rust with Actix Web, each endpoint is typically implemented as an asynchronous handler function tied to one of these methods.

Project Structure

As projects grow, structure becomes essential. Here's a scalable layout:

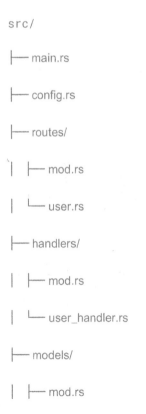

```
src/

├── main.rs

├── config.rs

├── routes/

│   ├── mod.rs

│   └── user.rs

├── handlers/

│   ├── mod.rs

│   └── user_handler.rs

├── models/

│   ├── mod.rs
```

```
|   └── user.rs

├── services/

|   ├── mod.rs

|   └── user_service.rs
```

This modular structure separates concerns and allows for cleaner testing, mocking, and maintenance.

Building a Simple User API

Let's walk through a CRUD API for managing users. Start by adding dependencies in `Cargo.toml`:

```toml
[dependencies]

actix-web = "4"

serde = { version = "1", features = ["derive"] }

serde_json = "1"

tokio = { version = "1", features = ["full"] }

uuid = { version = "1", features = ["v4"] }
```

Defining the User Model

```rust
use serde::{Deserialize, Serialize};

use uuid::Uuid;
```

```rust
#[derive(Serialize, Deserialize, Clone)]

pub struct User {

    pub id: Uuid,

    pub name: String,

    pub email: String,

}
```

Creating a Handler

Handlers process HTTP requests. Here's a set of handlers for basic user operations:

```rust
use actix_web::{get, post, put, delete, web, HttpResponse,
Responder};

use uuid::Uuid;

use crate::models::user::User;

use std::sync::Mutex;


type Db = web::Data<Mutex<Vec<User>>>;


#[get("/users")]

async fn get_users(db: Db) -> impl Responder {

    let users = db.lock().unwrap();

    HttpResponse::Ok().json(&*users)

}
```

```rust
#[get("/users/{id}")]

async fn get_user(id: web::Path<Uuid>, db: Db) -> impl Responder {

    let users = db.lock().unwrap();

    match users.iter().find(|u| u.id == *id) {

        Some(user) => HttpResponse::Ok().json(user),

        None => HttpResponse::NotFound().finish(),

    }

}


#[post("/users")]

async fn create_user(new_user: web::Json<User>, db: Db) -> impl
Responder {

    let mut users = db.lock().unwrap();

    users.push(new_user.into_inner());

    HttpResponse::Created().finish()

}


#[delete("/users/{id}")]

async fn delete_user(id: web::Path<Uuid>, db: Db) -> impl Responder
{

    let mut users = db.lock().unwrap();

    users.retain(|u| u.id != *id);

    HttpResponse::Ok().finish()

}
```

Connecting the Handlers in main.rs

```rust
use actix_web::{App, HttpServer, web};

use std::sync::Mutex;

use uuid::Uuid;

use crate::models::user::User;


mod models;

mod handlers;


#[actix_web::main]

async fn main() -> std::io::Result<()> {

    let user_data = web::Data::new(Mutex::new(vec![

        User {

            id: Uuid::new_v4(),

            name: "Alice".to_string(),

            email: "alice@example.com".to_string(),

        },

    ]));


    HttpServer::new(move || {

        App::new()

            .app_data(user_data.clone())
```

```
                    .service(handlers::user_handler::get_users)

                    .service(handlers::user_handler::get_user)

                    .service(handlers::user_handler::create_user)

                    .service(handlers::user_handler::delete_user)

    })

    .bind("127.0.0.1:8080")?

    .run()

    .await

}
```

This is a basic but complete RESTful API for managing user records.

Validation and Error Handling

Rust encourages type safety, but you still need to validate user input:

```
use validator::Validate;


#[derive(Deserialize, Validate)]

struct NewUser {

    #[validate(length(min = 3))]

    name: String,


    #[validate(email)]

    email: String,

}
```

You can return `Result<HttpResponse, actix_web::Error>` and use custom error responses:

```rust
use actix_web::{error, HttpResponse, ResponseError};
use derive_more::Display;

#[derive(Debug, Display)]
enum ApiError {
    #[display(fmt = "Validation error: {}", _0)]
    ValidationError(String),
}

impl ResponseError for ApiError {
    fn error_response(&self) -> HttpResponse {
        match self {
            ApiError::ValidationError(msg) =>
HttpResponse::BadRequest().body(msg),
        }
    }
}
```

Authentication and Authorization

Authentication can be added using JWT (JSON Web Tokens). Add `jsonwebtoken` to your dependencies:

```
jsonwebtoken = "9"
```

Define claims and generate tokens:

```
use jsonwebtoken::{encode, decode, Header, EncodingKey, DecodingKey, Validation};

use serde::{Serialize, Deserialize};


#[derive(Serialize, Deserialize)]

struct Claims {

    sub: String,

    exp: usize,

}
```

You can now sign and verify tokens and use middleware to protect routes.

Structuring Microservices

Each microservice should be:

- Independently deployable

- Focused on a single domain

- Communicating over HTTP, gRPC, or message queues

For example:

- auth-service: Handles registration, login, and token issuance

- `user-service`: CRUD operations for user data

- `mail-service`: Sends confirmation and alert emails

- `product-service`: Manages products or inventory

Each service can use Actix or any other framework and expose its API via REST.

Service Discovery and Load Balancing

In production environments, services need to find each other. This can be done via:

- DNS (Kubernetes service names)

- Service registries (Consul, etcd)

- API gateways (NGINX, Envoy)

You may use tools like `traefik` or `kong` to manage traffic and secure endpoints.

Testing and Documentation

REST APIs must be tested using integration tools such as:

- `reqwest` or `actix-web::test` for internal tests

- Postman or Insomnia for manual testing

- Swagger/OpenAPI for documentation

Actix supports automatic testing:

```
#[actix_web::test]

async fn test_get_users() {

    let data = web::Data::new(Mutex::new(vec![]));
```

```
    let app =
test::init_service(App::new().app_data(data.clone()).service(get_use
rs)).await;

    let req = test::TestRequest::get().uri("/users").to_request();

    let resp = test::call_service(&app, req).await;

    assert_eq!(resp.status(), 200);

}
```

CI/CD and Deployment

Once you have a working API, the next step is automated testing and deployment:

- Use GitHub Actions or GitLab CI to build and test

- Create Docker containers for each service

- Use orchestration tools like Kubernetes or Docker Compose

Example Dockerfile:

```
FROM rust:1.73 as builder

WORKDIR /app

COPY . .

RUN cargo build --release


FROM debian:buster-slim

COPY --from=builder /app/target/release/my-api /usr/local/bin/my-api

CMD ["my-api"]
```

Conclusion

Building REST APIs and microservices in Rust with Actix Web provides performance, safety, and modern async support. You've seen how to:

- Create a scalable project structure

- Implement CRUD operations

- Validate input and handle errors

- Add authentication via JWT

- Structure your system into microservices

This foundation enables you to build anything from internal APIs to internet-scale services. In the next section, we'll explore WebAssembly (WASM) and how to use Rust beyond the server to power web clients and edge functions.

WebAssembly (WASM) and Rust

WebAssembly (WASM) is a low-level, binary instruction format that allows high-performance code to run on the web and in other environments such as servers, IoT, and embedded devices. Rust is one of the best languages for compiling to WASM, thanks to its strong focus on safety, speed, and its close-to-the-metal capabilities. This section explores how to use Rust to build WebAssembly modules, integrate them into web apps, and run them in a variety of runtime environments.

We'll go deep into the toolchain, module architecture, memory management, interoperability with JavaScript, and use-cases like frontend UI rendering, background processing, and WASM on the server.

Why Rust + WASM?

Rust is uniquely positioned to work well with WASM due to:

- Zero-cost abstractions

- Strong compile-time guarantees

- Small and predictable binary size

- Excellent tooling (e.g., `wasm-pack`, `wasm-bindgen`, `cargo install`)

- Interoperability with JS via bindings

Use cases include:

- High-performance browser applications

- CPU-intensive workloads (e.g., games, simulations)

- Porting native libraries to the web

- Serverless or edge computing

Toolchain Setup

To build Rust code into WASM, you need the following tools:

1. **wasm32-unknown-unknown** target

2. **wasm-pack** for bundling and publishing

3. **wasm-bindgen** for bridging Rust and JS

Install them:

```
rustup target add wasm32-unknown-unknown

cargo install wasm-pack
```

Hello, WASM in Rust

Let's create a basic WASM module that exports a function.

```
cargo new --lib wasm_greeter
```

```
cd wasm_greeter
```

Edit `Cargo.toml`:

```
[package]
name = "wasm_greeter"
version = "0.1.0"
edition = "2021"

[lib]
crate-type = ["cdylib"]

[dependencies]
wasm-bindgen = "0.2"
```

Update `src/lib.rs`:

```rust
use wasm_bindgen::prelude::*;

#[wasm_bindgen]
pub fn greet(name: &str) -> String {
    format!("Hello, {}!", name)
}
```

Now build and package it:

```
wasm-pack build --target web
```

This outputs a pkg/ directory containing the .wasm file and JS bindings.

Integrating with HTML/JS

Create a simple HTML file:

```html
<!DOCTYPE html>

<html>

<head>

    <meta charset="utf-8">

    <title>Rust WASM Greet</title>

</head>

<body>

    <input id="name" />

    <button onclick="sayHello()">Greet</button>

    <p id="output"></p>


    <script type="module">

        import init, { greet } from './pkg/wasm_greeter.js';


        async function sayHello() {

            await init();

            const name = document.getElementById("name").value;
```

```
        const output = greet(name);

        document.getElementById("output").innerText = output;

    }

</script>

</body>

</html>
```

Serve this with a static server (e.g., `python3 -m http.server`) and open in your browser.

Understanding wasm-bindgen

`wasm-bindgen` is the glue between Rust and JavaScript. It generates bindings so JS can call Rust functions and vice versa. You can export more than just strings:

```
#[wasm_bindgen]

pub fn add(a: i32, b: i32) -> i32 {

    a + b

}
```

It also supports structs, classes, and invoking JS APIs from Rust:

```
#[wasm_bindgen]

extern "C" {

    fn alert(s: &str);

}
```

```rust
#[wasm_bindgen]

pub fn welcome_user(name: &str) {

    alert(&format!("Welcome, {}!", name));

}
```

Memory Management and Performance

WASM modules have their own linear memory, separate from JS. Sharing data is more efficient with numeric types; strings and complex objects require serialization and copying.

Use `wasm-bindgen` features like `JsValue`, `serde`, and `into_serde` for efficient interop:

```rust
use wasm_bindgen::JsValue;

use serde::{Serialize, Deserialize};


#[derive(Serialize, Deserialize)]

struct User {

    name: String,

    age: u32,

}


#[wasm_bindgen]

pub fn process_user(data: &JsValue) -> Result<JsValue, JsValue> {

    let user: User = data.into_serde().map_err(|e|
JsValue::from_str(&e.to_string()))?;

    let new_user = User { name: user.name.to_uppercase(), age:
user.age + 1 };
```

```
    JsValue::from_serde(&new_user).map_err(|e|
JsValue::from_str(&e.to_string()))

}
```

Using `wee_alloc` for Smaller Binaries

By default, Rust uses the system allocator. For smaller WASM binaries, use `wee_alloc`:

```
[dependencies]

wee_alloc = "0.4"
```

```
[lib]

crate-type = ["cdylib"]
```

```
[profile.release]

opt-level = "z"

lto = true
```

In `lib.rs`:

```
#[global_allocator]

static ALLOC: wee_alloc::WeeAlloc = wee_alloc::WeeAlloc::INIT;
```

Building a Frontend App with Yew

Yew is a modern Rust framework for building single-page apps in WASM, similar to React.

Add to `Cargo.toml`:

```
[dependencies]
yew = "0.20"
wasm-bindgen = "0.2"
```

Example component:

```rust
use yew::prelude::*;

#[function_component(App)]
fn app() -> Html {
    let name = use_state(|| String::from("World"));
    let onclick = {
        let name = name.clone();
        Callback::from(move |_| name.set(String::from("Rustacean")))
    };

    html! {
        <>
            <h1>{ format!("Hello, {}!", *name) }</h1>
            <button onclick={onclick}>{ "Change Name" }</button>
        </>
    }
}
```

```
}
```

Yew apps are compiled to WASM and run entirely in the browser. They're great for performance-sensitive frontend logic.

WASM Outside the Browser

Rust+WASM isn't just for the web. You can use WASM on the server, in embedded systems, and for plugin architectures.

WASI

WASI (WebAssembly System Interface) allows WASM modules to access system-level features like file I/O and sockets, making it usable outside the browser.

Install WASI target:

```
rustup target add wasm32-wasi
```

Compile a Rust binary:

```
cargo build --target wasm32-wasi --release
```

Run it with wasmtime or wasmer:

```
wasmtime target/wasm32-wasi/release/my_wasm_app.wasm
```

Microservices with WASM

Some cloud platforms allow deploying serverless WASM functions (e.g., Cloudflare Workers, Fastly Compute@Edge, Fermyon Spin). These let you:

- Deploy tiny, fast-starting units of compute

- Share code across frontend and backend

- Write logic once and deploy anywhere

For example, a WASM-powered auth function can be embedded in both a browser app and a serverless edge function.

Debugging and Tooling

Debugging WASM isn't as easy as native Rust, but it's improving. Tools include:

- `wasm-pack test --headless --firefox`

- `console_error_panic_hook` for better panic messages

- Source maps for easier browser debugging

- `wasm-opt` from Binaryen for binary optimization

Add panic hooks to improve debug output:

```
#[wasm_bindgen(start)]

pub fn main() {

    console_error_panic_hook::set_once();

}
```

Publishing to npm

WASM modules compiled with `wasm-pack` can be published as npm packages:

```
wasm-pack build --target bundler
```

```
npm publish
```

You can then import them in JS/TS codebases like any other package.

Best Practices

- Minimize JS interop: cross-language calls are expensive

- Use efficient data formats (e.g., JSON, binary, FlatBuffers)

- Benchmark performance with `wasm-bindgen-test`

- Split large binaries using code-splitting or multiple modules

- Use `#[wasm_bindgen(skip)]` to avoid bloating the WASM interface

Conclusion

Rust and WebAssembly together empower developers to write safe, fast, and reusable code for the web and beyond. Whether you're building a frontend SPA with Yew, optimizing a JavaScript-heavy app with Rust modules, or deploying tiny microservices at the edge, WASM unlocks new capabilities for system-level Rust code to run in environments where native binaries aren't an option.

In the next chapter, we'll dive into performance optimization and debugging techniques that apply to both native and WASM-targeted Rust applications. You'll learn how to identify bottlenecks, reduce binary size, and get the most out of your Rust-based systems.

Chapter 9: Performance Optimization and Debugging

Profiling and Benchmarking Rust Code

Performance is one of Rust's core promises, but writing fast code is not just about choosing the right language—it's about making informed decisions based on actual data. Profiling and benchmarking are essential tools for identifying bottlenecks, understanding performance characteristics, and optimizing applications effectively. This section explores the philosophy, tools, and best practices for profiling and benchmarking Rust code.

The Need for Performance Analysis

Rust's zero-cost abstractions and ownership model encourage developers to write efficient code. However, real-world applications often include complex logic, third-party dependencies, and unpredictable usage patterns. Guessing where performance issues lie is risky. The human mind is notoriously bad at estimating what part of code takes the most time. That's where profiling and benchmarking step in:

- **Profiling** helps identify *where* the time is being spent.

- **Benchmarking** helps measure *how fast* or *slow* a specific operation or function is.

Together, these techniques provide the empirical foundation for meaningful performance tuning.

Benchmarking Rust Code

Benchmarking is about measuring the runtime of small units of code in a consistent, repeatable environment. Rust offers several tools for this:

Using `cargo bench`

Rust provides built-in support for benchmarking via the unstable `test` crate, which requires a nightly compiler.

Steps:

Switch to nightly:

sh

```
rustup override set nightly
```

1.

Add the following to your `Cargo.toml`:

toml

```toml
[dev-dependencies]
criterion = "0.5"
```

2.

Create a `benches` folder and add a benchmark file:

rust

```rust
// benches/my_benchmark.rs
use criterion::{black_box, criterion_group, criterion_main, Criterion};


fn fibonacci(n: u64) -> u64 {
    match n {
        0 => 0,
        1 => 1,
        _ => fibonacci(n - 1) + fibonacci(n - 2),
    }
}


fn bench_fibonacci(c: &mut Criterion) {
    c.bench_function("fibonacci 20", |b| b.iter(||
fibonacci(black_box(20))));
}


criterion_group!(benches, bench_fibonacci);
```

```
criterion_main!(benches);
```

   3.

Run the benchmark:

sh

```
cargo bench
```

   4.

This will output detailed performance statistics, including mean execution time, standard deviation, and more.

Criterion.rs

Criterion is the de facto benchmarking library for Rust due to its statistical rigor. It avoids common benchmarking pitfalls like CPU frequency scaling and OS jitter. It also generates detailed HTML reports.

Key benefits:

- Automatic outlier detection

- Statistical significance testing

- Regression tracking

Use `black_box` to prevent the compiler from optimizing away computations.

```
let result = black_box(some_expensive_function());
```

Profiling Rust Applications

Profiling tools help developers see the *runtime behavior* of their applications. Instead of guessing where CPU time is spent, a profiler will measure it.

`perf` on Linux

One of the most powerful profilers for Rust on Linux is `perf`. It provides call graphs, sample counts, and assembly-level details.

Steps:

Compile with debug symbols and optimizations:

sh

```
cargo build --release
```

1.

Run `perf`:

sh

```
perf record ./target/release/your_binary
```

2.

Generate a report:

sh

```
perf report
```

3.

For better symbols and demangling, install `rustfilt`:

```
cargo install rustfilt
```

Use:

```
perf script | rustfilt | less
```

flamegraph

`flamegraph` creates visual stack traces showing which functions consume the most CPU time.

Steps:

Install dependencies:

sh

```
cargo install flamegraph

sudo apt install linux-tools-common linux-tools-generic
```

1.

Run:

sh

```
cargo flamegraph
```

2.
3. Open the generated `flamegraph.svg` in a browser.

Using `Valgrind` and `Callgrind`

For deep profiling:

```
valgrind --tool=callgrind ./target/release/your_binary
```

Then visualize with tools like KCachegrind or QCachegrind.

Common Performance Pitfalls

Rust encourages fast code, but it's still easy to introduce slowdowns:

Unnecessary cloning: Cloning is cheap-looking but can be expensive for large data structures.

Bad:

rust

```
let data = expensive_data.clone();
```

Better:

rust

```
let data = &expensive_data;
```

-

- **Excessive heap allocations:** Favor stack-based storage when possible. Avoid frequent `Vec::push` on growing arrays—pre-allocate with `Vec::with_capacity`.

- **Inefficient iterators:** Iterators are powerful but can chain into inefficiencies if not used carefully.

- **Boxing dynamic traits:** Boxed trait objects (`Box<dyn Trait>`) are flexible but come with indirection and dynamic dispatch overhead.

- **Mutex contention:** In concurrent code, overusing mutexes can cause thread contention. Consider `RwLock` or atomics for read-heavy workloads.

Writing Benchmark-Friendly Code

To enable efficient benchmarking:

- **Modularize logic**: Write small functions that isolate behavior for easy benchmarking.

- **Avoid global state**: It interferes with test isolation and result reproducibility.

- **Make deterministic operations**: Reduce randomness or IO in benchmarked functions.

A good example:

```rust
pub fn sort_numbers(mut nums: Vec<i32>) -> Vec<i32> {

    nums.sort();

    nums

}
```

Now you can benchmark `sort_numbers` easily without worrying about side effects.

Profiling Memory Usage

Though Rust has no garbage collector, memory profiling is still important:

- Use `valgrind --tool=massif` to track heap usage.

- Use `heaptrack` for detailed allocation information.

- Check for memory leaks with `valgrind` or use the `leak` crate in test scenarios.

Benchmarking Asynchronous Code

Criterion now supports benchmarking async code using the `futures` crate. For example:

```rust
use criterion::{criterion_group, criterion_main, Criterion};
use tokio::runtime::Runtime;


async fn async_op() {
    // Simulate some async task
}


fn bench_async(c: &mut Criterion) {
    let rt = Runtime::new().unwrap();
    c.bench_function("async op", |b| {
        b.to_async(&rt).iter(|| async_op())
    });
}


criterion_group!(benches, bench_async);
criterion_main!(benches);
```

This allows async Rust functions to be benchmarked in isolation and under load.

Tips for Interpreting Benchmark Results

- **Ignore single runs**: Use averages and consider variance.

- **Warm up your code**: Run it a few times before measuring.

- **Automate regression checks**: Integrate with CI to prevent performance regressions.

- **Keep changes isolated**: When optimizing, change one thing at a time.

Integration with CI/CD

For long-term projects, integrate performance checks into your pipeline:

- Use Criterion with GitHub Actions.

- Export JSON/CSV data and graph trends over time.

- Fail builds on performance regression thresholds.

Summary

Profiling and benchmarking are critical to writing high-performance Rust applications. Rust gives you powerful tools, but they require deliberate usage. Use profiling tools like `perf`, `flamegraph`, and `valgrind` to understand your application's runtime behavior. Use Criterion to write reliable and statistically sound benchmarks. Avoid common performance traps like unnecessary cloning and mutex contention. And finally, let data guide your optimization decisions—not guesswork.

By embracing these practices, you can ensure your Rust applications not only compile without errors but also perform at world-class speed and efficiency.

Common Performance Pitfalls and Fixes

Rust is known for performance, safety, and control over system resources. However, even in a language as disciplined as Rust, developers can fall into subtle traps that degrade performance. This section identifies common performance issues and explains how to fix or avoid them. These examples cover everything from CPU-bound problems to memory inefficiencies, concurrency missteps, and poor abstraction design.

Unnecessary Heap Allocations

Rust encourages ownership and allocation through constructs like `Box`, `Vec`, and `String`, which can lead to excessive heap usage. Heap allocations are slower than stack allocations and often lead to fragmentation, increased pressure on the memory allocator, and reduced cache locality.

Example: Excessive Allocation

```rust
fn build_string() -> String {

    let mut s = String::new();

    for _ in 0..10_000 {

        s.push_str("data");

    }

    s

}
```

Every call to `push_str` may trigger a reallocation if the underlying buffer is not big enough.

Fix: Pre-allocate Memory

```rust
fn build_string() -> String {

    let mut s = String::with_capacity(40_000); // Estimate capacity

    for _ in 0..10_000 {

        s.push_str("data");

    }

    s

}
```

Avoiding dynamic reallocation drastically improves performance. The same principle applies to `Vec` and other collections.

Cloning Instead of Borrowing

The ease of using `.clone()` in Rust can become a performance pitfall. While cloning is often necessary, it may result in unnecessary deep copies.

Example: Cloning a Vector

```
fn process_data(data: Vec<i32>) {

    let copy = data.clone();

    // process copy

}
```

If the original data isn't reused, cloning is wasteful.

Fix: Use Ownership or References

```
fn process_data(data: Vec<i32>) {

    // Take ownership directly

    // process data

}
```

Or:

```
fn process_data(data: &[i32]) {

    // Borrow without cloning

}
```

Prefer references or ownership where appropriate, and reserve cloning for when it's truly necessary.

Overusing Dynamic Dispatch

Rust supports both static and dynamic dispatch. While dynamic dispatch via `dyn Trait` adds flexibility, it incurs runtime cost due to vtable lookups and heap allocations when used with `Box`.

Example: Dynamic Dispatch

```rust
trait Drawable {

    fn draw(&self);

}


fn render(shape: &Box<dyn Drawable>) {

    shape.draw();

}
```

Fix: Prefer Generics and Monomorphization

```rust
fn render<T: Drawable>(shape: &T) {

    shape.draw();

}
```

Generics allow the compiler to optimize calls at compile time. Use trait objects (`dyn`) only when heterogeneous types must be handled uniformly.

Inefficient Iterators and Loops

Iterators are idiomatic in Rust, but poor usage can lead to suboptimal performance.

Example: Nested `.map().collect().into_iter()`

```rust
let doubled: Vec<_> = vec![1, 2, 3]
```

```
    .iter()

    .map(|x| x * 2)

    .collect::<Vec<_>>()

    .into_iter()

    .collect();
```

This pattern causes intermediate allocation that can often be eliminated.

Fix: Avoid Intermediate Collections

```
let doubled: Vec<_> = vec![1, 2, 3]

    .iter()

    .map(|x| x * 2)

    .collect();
```

Or:

```
for x in vec![1, 2, 3].iter().map(|x| x * 2) {

    println!("{}", x);

}
```

Use lazy iteration chains and avoid unnecessary `.collect()` calls unless you truly need a collection.

Mutex Contention and Concurrency Bottlenecks

Rust makes concurrency safer, but not always faster. Using `Mutex` incorrectly can serialize operations, leading to contention and performance loss.

Example: Shared Counter with Mutex

```rust
use std::sync::{Arc, Mutex};

use std::thread;


fn main() {

    let counter = Arc::new(Mutex::new(0));

    let mut handles = vec![];


    for _ in 0..10 {

        let counter = Arc::clone(&counter);

        let handle = thread::spawn(move || {

            let mut num = counter.lock().unwrap();

            *num += 1;

        });

        handles.push(handle);

    }


    for handle in handles {

        handle.join().unwrap();

    }

}
```

Each thread locks the mutex, performs the update, and releases it—one at a time.

Fix: Use Atomics for Simple Updates

```rust
use std::sync::atomic::{AtomicUsize, Ordering};

use std::sync::Arc;

use std::thread;


fn main() {

    let counter = Arc::new(AtomicUsize::new(0));

    let mut handles = vec![];


    for _ in 0..10 {

        let counter = Arc::clone(&counter);

        let handle = thread::spawn(move || {

            counter.fetch_add(1, Ordering::SeqCst);

        });

        handles.push(handle);

    }


    for handle in handles {

        handle.join().unwrap();

    }

}
```

For simple counters and booleans, `Atomic*` types are faster and lock-free.

Over-Engineering with Traits and Abstractions

Traits promote reuse and flexibility, but too many layers of abstraction can result in larger binaries and slower execution due to inlining barriers.

Example: Over-Abstraction

```rust
trait DoSomething {
    fn do_it(&self) -> String;
}


struct A;

struct B;


impl DoSomething for A {
    fn do_it(&self) -> String { "A".to_string() }
}


impl DoSomething for B {
    fn do_it(&self) -> String { "B".to_string() }
}


fn perform(d: &dyn DoSomething) {
    println!("{}", d.do_it());
}
```

Fix: Use Enums or Concrete Types When Possible

```rust
enum Doer {
    A,
```

```
        B,

}


impl Doer {

    fn do_it(&self) -> String {

        match self {

            Doer::A => "A".to_string(),

            Doer::B => "B".to_string(),

        }

    }

}
```

Enums avoid dynamic dispatch and enable exhaustive matching, improving performance and readability.

Ignoring Compiler Optimizations

Sometimes, performance issues arise because developers unknowingly prevent optimizations by doing things like using `panic!` in hot code paths or writing unreachable code.

Example: Panic in Critical Path

```
fn divide(a: i32, b: i32) -> i32 {

    if b == 0 {

        panic!("divide by zero");

    }

    a / b

}
```

Even with b != 0, the panic branch can inhibit certain optimizations.

Fix: Return Result

```rust
fn divide(a: i32, b: i32) -> Result<i32, &'static str> {

    if b == 0 {

        return Err("divide by zero");

    }

    Ok(a / b)

}
```

Using `Result` allows the compiler to optimize non-error paths more aggressively.

Misusing `unwrap()` and `expect()`

These functions panic on error and are commonly used in development. However, in production or critical sections, they can lead to catastrophic crashes.

Example:

```rust
let data = std::fs::read_to_string("config.toml").unwrap();
```

Fix: Use Proper Error Handling

```rust
let data = std::fs::read_to_string("config.toml")

    .unwrap_or_else(|err| {

        eprintln!("Failed to read config: {}", err);

        std::process::exit(1);
```

```
});
```

Better yet, propagate errors using ? in functions that return Result.

Not Leveraging SIMD or Low-Level Optimizations

Rust allows you to write high-level code, but also lets you drop to lower levels when performance demands it.

Example: Naive Vector Addition

```
fn add_vectors(a: &[f32], b: &[f32]) -> Vec<f32> {

    a.iter().zip(b).map(|(x, y)| x + y).collect()

}
```

Fix: Use Crates Like packed_simd **or** wide

```
use wide::f32x4;


fn add_vectors_simd(a: &[f32], b: &[f32]) -> Vec<f32> {
    let mut result = vec![0.0; a.len()];
    for i in (0..a.len()).step_by(4) {
        let va = f32x4::from_slice_unaligned(&a[i..]);
        let vb = f32x4::from_slice_unaligned(&b[i..]);
        let vr = va + vb;
        vr.write_to_slice_unaligned(&mut result[i..]);
    }
    result
```

```
}
```

SIMD enables batch processing of data with dramatic speedups in mathematical and multimedia applications.

Summary and Best Practices

- Avoid unnecessary cloning and heap allocations.

- Use references and lifetimes to manage memory efficiently.

- Prefer static dispatch over dynamic when performance matters.

- Profile mutex use—consider atomics for simple concurrency.

- Benchmark iterator chains and use lazy evaluation.

- Avoid abstraction overhead in hot paths.

- Don't use panics in performance-critical code.

- Integrate SIMD or FFI when high performance is essential.

By understanding these pitfalls and applying idiomatic fixes, you can ensure your Rust applications remain lean, fast, and scalable. Optimize only after measuring, and keep the balance between performance, readability, and maintainability.

Debugging Tools and Techniques

Debugging is a fundamental part of the development process. In a systems-level language like Rust, where you have fine-grained control over memory, concurrency, and resource management, having robust debugging strategies is crucial. Rust emphasizes safety and correctness through its type system and compiler checks, but once code compiles and runs, logic bugs, performance anomalies, and concurrency errors can still arise.

This section explores various debugging tools and techniques available in the Rust ecosystem. We'll cover traditional debuggers, logging, assertions, tracing, memory analyzers, concurrency debugging, and integration with editors/IDEs. Whether you're debugging a segfault or chasing down a logic bug, this guide will equip you with the practical know-how to tackle issues effectively.

Debugging Philosophy in Rust

Before diving into tools, it's important to understand Rust's design philosophy toward debugging:

- **Catch bugs at compile time:** The borrow checker, type system, and exhaustive pattern matching aim to eliminate entire classes of runtime bugs.

- **Make errors explicit:** Error handling with `Result` and `Option` helps surface exceptional states in structured ways.

- **Enable powerful runtime inspection:** Through macros like `dbg!`, `println!`, `assert!`, and third-party libraries.

Despite all this, not every bug can be caught at compile time. Logical errors, performance regressions, off-by-one mistakes, and deadlocks require runtime tools.

Traditional Debugging with GDB and LLDB

Rust integrates well with GDB and LLDB, the two primary debuggers on Unix-based systems and macOS respectively.

Enabling Debug Info

Compile with debug symbols using:

```
cargo build
```

By default, this adds debug symbols. You can ensure this explicitly in `Cargo.toml`:

```
[profile.dev]
debug = true


[profile.release]
debug = true  # Add this to allow debugging in release builds
```

Using GDB

```
gdb target/debug/your_binary
```

Typical GDB workflow:

```
break main

run

next

print my_variable

backtrace
```

Note: GDB doesn't demangle Rust function names by default. Install `rustfilt` to view readable function names:

```
cargo install rustfilt
```

Then use:

```
bt | rustfilt
```

Using LLDB (macOS)

```
lldb target/debug/your_binary
```

Common LLDB commands:

```
break set --name main

run
```

```
frame variable

thread backtrace
```

LLDB offers better integration with some IDEs like Xcode and VSCode on macOS.

The dbg! Macro

Rust provides a built-in macro, dbg!, for quick and dirty debugging.

```
fn main() {

    let x = 5;

    let y = dbg!(x * 2) + 1;

    dbg!(y);

}
```

Output:

```
[src/main.rs:3] x * 2 = 10

[src/main.rs:4] y = 11
```

Advantages:

- Shows file and line number.

- Returns the value passed in, making it chainable.

Disadvantages:

- Not suitable for production code.

- No formatting control.

Logging for Runtime Inspection

For production-grade debugging, use structured logging via the `log` crate.

```
[dependencies]
log = "0.4"
env_logger = "0.10"
```

```
use log::{info, warn, error};
use env_logger;

fn main() {
    env_logger::init();
    info!("App started");
    warn!("Low disk space");
    error!("Connection failed");
}
```

Control verbosity via environment variables:

```
RUST_LOG=info cargo run
```

Logging supports targets, modules, and filtered verbosity, enabling fine-grained inspection.

Assertions and Custom Panics

Use assertions to catch unexpected states:

```
assert!(value > 0);

assert_eq!(result, expected);
```

Use `debug_assert!` for checks that only run in debug mode:

```
debug_assert!(index < buffer.len());
```

You can also define custom panic hooks:

```
use std::panic;

fn main() {
    panic::set_hook(Box::new(|info| {
        eprintln!("Custom panic: {}", info);
    }));

    panic!("Something went wrong");
}
```

This allows logging or telemetry even during panics.

Tracing with `tracing`

`tracing` is a modern framework for structured, event-based diagnostics, especially useful in async or multi-threaded applications.

```
[dependencies]

tracing = "0.1"

tracing-subscriber = "0.3"
```

```
use tracing::{info, instrument};

use tracing_subscriber;
```

```
#[instrument]

fn my_func(x: u32) {

    info!("Processing {}", x);

}
```

```
fn main() {

    tracing_subscriber::fmt::init();

    my_func(42);

}
```

#[instrument] records function arguments and timing, which is invaluable for tracing execution across threads or tasks.

Backtraces and Panics

Rust can show stack traces when a panic occurs:

```
RUST_BACKTRACE=1 cargo run
```

Or full trace:

```
RUST_BACKTRACE=full cargo run
```

To inspect panics in unit tests:

```
RUST_BACKTRACE=1 cargo test
```

Panics include location and line number, helping pinpoint logic bugs or failed assumptions.

Memory Debugging

Despite Rust's memory safety guarantees, bugs can still occur in unsafe code, FFI, or via logic errors (e.g. double allocation, uninitialized reads).

Valgrind

```
valgrind ./target/debug/your_binary
```

Useful for:

- Detecting memory leaks

- Invalid reads/writes

- Use-after-free errors

Note: Valgrind requires debug symbols and performs best on simple binaries (not async-heavy).

Miri

Miri is an interpreter for Rust MIR (Mid-level Intermediate Representation). It detects:

- Undefined behavior

- Use-after-free

- Invalid pointer dereference

Install with:

```
rustup component add miri

cargo miri test
```

Miri is especially useful in unsafe-heavy code.

Concurrency Debugging

Race conditions and deadlocks are notoriously hard to debug. Rust's type system avoids many concurrency errors, but not all.

Deadlocks

A typical deadlock pattern:

```
let m1 = Arc::new(Mutex::new(1));

let m2 = Arc::new(Mutex::new(2));


let a = Arc::clone(&m1);

let b = Arc::clone(&m2);


let handle1 = thread::spawn(move || {

    let _lock1 = a.lock().unwrap();

    thread::sleep(Duration::from_secs(1));

    let _lock2 = b.lock().unwrap();

});
```

```
let handle2 = thread::spawn(move || {

    let _lock2 = m2.lock().unwrap();

    thread::sleep(Duration::from_secs(1));

    let _lock1 = m1.lock().unwrap();

});
```

Detect deadlocks by:

- Using logging to track lock acquisition order

- Running with tools like `loom` or `tokio-console` (for async)

`loom` for Deterministic Testing

Loom explores possible interleavings of concurrent code:

```
[dev-dependencies]
loom = "0.5"
```

```
use loom::sync::Mutex;

use loom::thread;
```

```
fn main() {

    loom::model(|| {

        let data = Arc::new(Mutex::new(0));
```

```
    let d1 = Arc::clone(&data);

    let d2 = Arc::clone(&data);


    let t1 = thread::spawn(move || {

        let mut val = d1.lock().unwrap();

        *val += 1;

    });


    let t2 = thread::spawn(move || {

        let mut val = d2.lock().unwrap();

        *val += 1;

    });


    t1.join().unwrap();

    t2.join().unwrap();

    });

}
```

Loom is slow but exhaustive, suitable for catching rare bugs.

Debugging Async Code

Async Rust can obscure stack traces due to future combinators and executors. Tools that help:

- `tokio-console`: Realtime tracing of tasks, spawn points, wakers.

- `tracing`: Emits spans and events that follow async execution paths.

- `cargo-instruments` **(macOS)**: Instrumentation for async tasks and CPU activity.

Also, write simpler sync analogs of async code for easier reasoning and unit testing.

IDE and Editor Integration

VSCode with `rust-analyzer` provides:

- Inline error and type hints

- Go-to-definition

- Debugger support with GDB/LLDB

- Integrated terminal and logging

JetBrains CLion and IntelliJ Rust also provide strong debugging tools and project navigation.

Debug Builds vs Release Builds

Debug builds prioritize debuggability over speed. Release builds enable optimizations that may reorder or inline code, making debugging harder.

Use:

```
cargo build --release
```

Only for final performance profiling. Most logic debugging should happen in debug mode with full symbol support.

To debug release builds:

```
[profile.release]
debug = true
```

Summary and Recommendations

- Use `dbg!` and `println!` for quick checks.

- Use `log`, `tracing`, and `env_logger` for structured runtime diagnostics.

- Leverage GDB/LLDB for breakpoints and stepwise inspection.

- Enable backtraces with `RUST_BACKTRACE`.

- Detect memory bugs with `valgrind` and `miri`.

- Avoid deadlocks via lock-ordering and tools like `loom`.

- Trace async apps using `tracing` and `tokio-console`.

- Keep debug symbols even in release builds for diagnostics.

- Favor reproducible tests, minimal examples, and incremental isolation of bugs.

Mastering these debugging techniques makes Rust development more predictable, less frustrating, and ultimately more productive. Even in the face of complex concurrency or low-level unsafe code, Rust's ecosystem equips you with the tools to fix what's broken, fast and confidently.

Writing High-Performance Rust Applications

Writing high-performance Rust applications goes beyond simply choosing a fast language. It requires a mindset and approach grounded in measurement, profiling, iteration, and design decisions that align with system-level thinking. Rust gives you powerful tools—zero-cost abstractions, fine-grained memory control, compile-time guarantees—but you must use them thoughtfully to deliver real-world speed, scalability, and responsiveness.

This section is a deep dive into the art and engineering of crafting fast, reliable, and resource-efficient Rust applications. We'll explore idiomatic performance patterns, architectural considerations, memory and concurrency strategies, and how to write and maintain performant code at scale.

Start with a Performance-Oriented Architecture

Before optimizing specific functions, the structure of your application should reflect performance goals. Here are some architectural tips:

- **Avoid unnecessary layers of abstraction.** Traits and generic indirection are powerful but introduce complexity and sometimes overhead.

- **Design data flow to minimize copying.** Data ownership and movement should be explicit and deliberate.

- **Defer expensive computation.** Lazy evaluation or caching strategies are often more impactful than micro-optimizations.

Rust's ownership model rewards thoughtful structuring. For example:

```rust
struct LargeData {
    buffer: Vec<u8>,
}

impl LargeData {
    fn new(size: usize) -> Self {
        Self {
            buffer: Vec::with_capacity(size),
        }
    }

    fn process(&mut self) {
        for byte in &mut self.buffer {
            *byte = byte.saturating_add(1);
        }
    }
}
```

By allocating up-front and modifying in-place, we maintain both performance and clarity.

Measure First, Optimize Second

Optimization without measurement is wasted effort. Rust provides multiple ways to measure:

- `cargo bench` with `criterion` for precise benchmarks

- `perf`, `flamegraph`, and `valgrind` for profiling

- `tracing` and `tokio-console` for concurrent/async inspection

Integrate benchmarks into your development cycle and use them to track regressions.

```rust
use criterion::{black_box, criterion_group, criterion_main,
Criterion};


fn heavy_compute(n: u64) -> u64 {

    (1..=n).fold(0, |acc, x| acc + x)

}


fn bench_compute(c: &mut Criterion) {

    c.bench_function("heavy_compute", |b| b.iter(||
heavy_compute(black_box(10_000))));

}


criterion_group!(benches, bench_compute);

criterion_main!(benches);
```

Use Efficient Data Structures

Choose the right collection for the task. Rust's standard library includes `Vec`, `HashMap`, `BTreeMap`, `HashSet`, and others, each with different performance tradeoffs.

- Vec is great for contiguous storage and fast iteration.

- HashMap offers O(1) average lookup time but is cache-unfriendly.

- BTreeMap is slower for small keys but more cache-friendly and supports ordered traversal.

Example:

```
use std::collections::HashMap;


let mut map = HashMap::new();

map.insert("alpha", 1);

map.insert("beta", 2);
```

Avoid premature generalization. Use concrete types (Vec<T>) instead of trait objects (Box<dyn Collection>) unless flexibility is absolutely necessary.

Optimize Memory Usage

Memory efficiency affects speed via cache usage and allocation overhead. Tips:

- Prefer stack over heap: use arrays or small structs.

- Avoid excessive boxing: use Box<T> only when size or recursion demands it.

- Reduce allocation churn: reuse buffers, pre-allocate with with_capacity.

Example: instead of reallocating with every push:

```
let mut v = Vec::new();

for _ in 0..1_000 {

    v.push(42);
```

```
}
```

Use:

```
let mut v = Vec::with_capacity(1_000);
```

Also, consider using `SmallVec` or `arrayvec` for stack-backed vectors when the data is usually small.

Cache Locality and Loop Optimization

Modern CPUs are fast, but memory access is often the bottleneck. Good locality leads to significant gains.

Example: Iterating with contiguous memory access:

```
let mut sum = 0;

for i in 0..1_000_000 {

    sum += i;

}
```

This is fast due to linear memory access and prefetching.

Avoid scattered memory patterns such as linked lists or random hash lookups in performance-critical loops.

Eliminate Redundant Computation

Identify repeated work that can be factored out, memoized, or precomputed.

Bad:

```
for item in list.iter() {

    let result = expensive_fn(item);
```

```
    process(result);

}
```

If `expensive_fn` is pure and deterministic, memoize it:

```
let mut cache = HashMap::new();

for item in list.iter() {

    let result = cache.entry(item.clone()).or_insert_with(||
expensive_fn(item));

    process(*result);

}
```

Memoization is especially useful in recursive computations like Fibonacci or parsing.

Concurrency and Parallelism

Rust excels at parallel programming, but the key is choosing the right concurrency model:

- **Multi-threaded CPU-bound work:** Use `rayon` or explicit thread pools.

- **Async I/O-bound work:** Use `tokio` or `async-std`.

Using Rayon

```
use rayon::prelude::*;


let nums: Vec<u32> = (0..1_000_000).collect();

let squares: Vec<_> = nums.par_iter().map(|n| n * n).collect();
```

`par_iter()` enables parallel iteration with minimal changes to sequential logic.

Async with Tokio

```
use tokio::task;


#[tokio::main]

async fn main() {

    let handles: Vec<_> = (0..10).map(|_| {

        task::spawn(async {

            // Async I/O work

        })

    }).collect();


    for handle in handles {

        handle.await.unwrap();

    }

}
```

Avoid blocking calls in async tasks. Use `.await` responsibly and offload CPU work to dedicated threads when needed.

Writing Hot Path Code

Code that runs frequently should be kept simple, predictable, and branch-optimized.

Avoid:

- Deep call chains

- Trait object indirection

- Complex match patterns

- Allocations inside loops

Do:

- Inline small functions

- Use `#[inline(always)]` on hot functions (with caution)

- Unroll tight loops manually if necessary

- Leverage SIMD where appropriate (via `wide` or `packed_simd` crates)

Example:

```
#[inline(always)]
fn fast_add(a: i32, b: i32) -> i32 {
    a + b
}
```

Use `cargo asm` to inspect assembly and ensure optimizations are applied.

Error Handling Without Overhead

Idiomatic error handling in Rust uses `Result` and ?, but excessive chaining or match branching can affect performance in critical code.

In tight loops:

- Pre-validate outside the loop to reduce error handling inside.

- Use `unwrap_unchecked()` (nightly only) if you are **absolutely** sure the value is valid and want to eliminate bounds checks.

```
unsafe {
```

```
    let value = some_option.unwrap_unchecked();

}
```

This is dangerous and should be backed by exhaustive precondition checking.

Continuous Performance Testing

Once performance is achieved, it must be preserved. Integrate performance testing into CI/CD:

- Use Criterion with historical tracking.

- Compare against baseline results in JSON/CSV.

- Fail builds on regressions above a threshold.

Example: Automating in GitHub Actions:

```
- name: Run Benchmarks

  run: cargo bench -- --output-format bencher | tee output.txt
```

You can parse this with a custom script or compare mean values for critical paths.

Use Efficient Parsing and Serialization

For networked or file-based applications, parsing and serialization performance can dominate.

Avoid:

- JSON for high-throughput communication

- XML unless strictly required

Prefer:

- bincode for compact binary formats

- `postcard` for embedded systems

- `serde_json` only when human readability is necessary

Example:

```
use bincode;
use serde::{Serialize, Deserialize};


#[derive(Serialize, Deserialize)]
struct Data {
    id: u32,
    name: String,
}


let encoded = bincode::serialize(&data).unwrap();
let decoded: Data = bincode::deserialize(&encoded).unwrap();
```

Binary formats are significantly faster to parse and serialize.

Using Unsafe for Speed (Carefully)

Rust allows unsafe code when absolutely necessary for performance. Use `unsafe` to:

- Bypass bounds checks

- Access low-level system interfaces

- Interface with C or SIMD intrinsics

Only write unsafe code when:

- It can be isolated and encapsulated

- Safety invariants are clearly documented

- It has thorough test coverage and Miri validation

Example:

```
unsafe {

    let ptr = my_vec.as_ptr().add(5);

    let val = *ptr;

}
```

Verify with `cargo miri test`.

Summary and Checklist

To write high-performance Rust applications:

- Architect with data and ownership flow in mind.

- Measure before you optimize.

- Choose collections that fit your access patterns.

- Minimize allocations and prefer reuse.

- Leverage concurrency with Rayon and Tokio.

- Keep hot paths minimal and branch-free.

- Serialize with binary formats for speed.

- Use `unsafe` only with great care and justification.

- Integrate performance regression testing in CI.

Rust is capable of delivering C-like performance without sacrificing safety, but it requires a conscious performance discipline. With the right tools, practices, and design principles, you can build applications that not only compile, but compete—at scale, and in production.

Chapter 10: Rust in Production: Best Practices

Writing Maintainable and Scalable Rust Code

Writing production-grade Rust code is about more than just getting the compiler to accept your program. It's about building systems that are reliable, understandable, extensible, and efficient at scale. This section dives into strategies and tools to make your Rust codebases maintainable and scalable — two critical qualities for long-term software success in professional environments.

Embracing Idiomatic Rust

Writing idiomatic Rust is the first step toward maintainable code. Rust has its own set of conventions that differ from other languages. Following these idioms makes your code easier to read and collaborate on.

- Prefer `match` and pattern matching for exhaustive control flow.

- Use `Option` and `Result` instead of nulls or exceptions.

- Leverage the ownership system to prevent shared mutable state.

- Avoid unnecessary use of `unsafe` unless performance-critical and audited.

Idiomatic code aligns with the expectations of the Rust ecosystem, making it easier for other developers to understand and modify your work.

```rust
fn find_username(id: u32) -> Option<String> {

    let usernames = vec!["Alice", "Bob", "Carol"];

    usernames.get(id as usize).map(|&name| name.to_string())

}
```

In this simple function, we use safe indexing with `get` and transform the result with `map`—a common idiom in Rust.

Structuring Your Codebase

Organizing your code into modules and crates improves readability and scalability. Rust encourages a modular structure using the mod keyword for logical grouping and reusability.

- Keep files small and focused.

- Group related functionality in modules.

- Use libraries and crates to separate concerns.

For large applications, adopt a layered structure:

- **domain** (business logic)

- **application** (orchestrates domain and infrastructure)

- **infrastructure** (IO, networking, DB)

- **presentation** (CLI, web API, GUI)

Example project layout:

```
src/

├── main.rs

├── lib.rs

├── domain/

│   └── user.rs

├── infrastructure/

│   └── db.rs

├── application/

│   └── handlers.rs

└── presentation/
```

```
└── http.rs
```

This structure helps with testing, team collaboration, and long-term maintenance.

Error Handling Strategies

Rust's type system enforces error handling at compile time, which is a strength when aiming for scalable and robust systems.

Result and Error Enums

Create custom error types using enums and implement From or thiserror for automatic conversions.

```rust
use std::fs::File;

use std::io::{self, Read};

use thiserror::Error;


#[derive(Error, Debug)]

pub enum MyError {

    #[error("I/O error")]

    Io(#[from] io::Error),


    #[error("Invalid format")]

    FormatError,

}


fn read_file() -> Result<String, MyError> {

    let mut file = File::open("config.txt")?;
```

```
    let mut contents = String::new();

    file.read_to_string(&mut contents)?;

    Ok(contents)

}
```

By unifying error handling into a single error enum, your code becomes easier to debug and reason about.

Error Propagation

Use `?` to bubble up errors and keep functions concise and focused. For long chains of operations, consider breaking them into small functions with clear responsibilities.

Testing for Maintainability

Testing is crucial in production environments, and Rust makes it easy to write fast, safe, and expressive tests.

- Use `#[cfg(test)]` and `#[test]` to write unit tests.

- Group integration tests in the `tests/` directory.

- Mock dependencies using traits or external crates like `mockall`.

```
#[cfg(test)]

mod tests {

    use super::*;


    #[test]

    fn test_find_username() {

        assert_eq!(find_username(1), Some("Bob".to_string()));

    }
```

```
}
```

For testability:

- Avoid global state.

- Use dependency injection via traits.

- Write fast and deterministic tests.

Documentation and Comments

Clear documentation is a long-term investment that pays off when onboarding new developers or returning to your code months later.

Use Rustdoc comments (///) generously:

```
/// Finds a username by ID.

///

/// Returns `None` if the ID is out of range.

fn find_username(id: u32) -> Option<String> {

    ...

}
```

Generate documentation using `cargo doc` and host it internally for teams to browse easily.

Dependency Management

Rust's `Cargo.toml` makes managing dependencies straightforward. For scalable projects:

- Avoid overusing dependencies—prefer the standard library when possible.

- Audit dependencies for security issues using `cargo audit`.

- Use `cargo update` and `cargo outdated` regularly to maintain healthy packages.

Pin specific versions when needed, especially in production environments where reproducibility matters.

```
[dependencies]

serde = "1.0"

tokio = { version = "1", features = ["full"] }
```

Group dependencies logically and remove unused ones to keep the project lean.

Performance and Profiling

Scalability isn't just about code size—it's about performance under load. Rust's zero-cost abstractions help, but profiling is essential for real-world scenarios.

Use tools like:

- `cargo bench` for benchmarking

- `perf`, `valgrind`, or `dhat` for memory profiling

- `flamegraph` for visual performance bottlenecks

Benchmark critical paths and refactor hot code accordingly:

```
#[bench]

fn bench_sort(b: &mut test::Bencher) {

    let mut vec = (0..1000).rev().collect::<Vec<_>>();

    b.iter(|| vec.sort());

}
```

Avoid premature optimization, but always measure before refactoring.

Code Reviews and Linting

Peer reviews and automated linting improve code quality at scale.

Use Clippy:

```
cargo clippy
```

And integrate formatting checks:

```
cargo fmt --check
```

For CI, enforce checks to block regressions before merge. Educate teams on reviewing Rust-specific patterns, like ownership flow and lifetime annotations.

Version Control and Branching Strategy

Use Git effectively:

- Keep `main` or `master` stable.

- Use feature branches for development.

- Consider `trunk-based development` or `GitFlow`, depending on team preference.

Use semantic commit messages and automated tools for changelog generation (e.g., `conventional-changelog`).

Example commit:

```
feat(domain): add validation to user registration
```

Continuous Integration Setup

Set up CI pipelines using GitHub Actions, GitLab CI, or others. Include:

- cargo check

- cargo test

- cargo fmt

- cargo clippy

- cargo audit

Example GitHub Actions snippet:

```
jobs:
  test:
    runs-on: ubuntu-latest
    steps:
      - uses: actions/checkout@v3
      - name: Install Rust
        uses: actions-rs/toolchain@v1
        with:
          toolchain: stable
      - name: Run tests
        run: cargo test --all
```

Automating these checks guarantees code health across environments.

Scaling Teams and Collaboration

As teams grow, maintaining Rust projects requires clear coding standards, documentation, and tooling support. Establish shared style guides, create onboarding documentation, and use internal tooling to enforce best practices.

Invest in developer experience:

- Use IDE extensions (e.g., rust-analyzer)

- Set up fast builds with `sccache`

- Use `cargo-watch` for hot reloads during dev

Encourage internal talks, shared libraries, and community involvement to spread Rust expertise.

Conclusion

Maintainable and scalable Rust code isn't just about syntax or performance—it's about the ecosystem you build around your codebase. Idiomatic patterns, modular organization, strong testing, documentation, and tooling combine to form robust systems that evolve gracefully. By embracing these best practices, teams can build long-lived Rust systems that remain fast, safe, and delightful to work with.

Security Best Practices in Rust

Security is a first-class concern in any production-grade system, and Rust's strong memory safety model provides a powerful foundation for writing secure software. However, memory safety alone is not sufficient. Security spans across application logic, dependency management, cryptographic correctness, secure coding practices, and deployment considerations. In this section, we explore how to leverage Rust's strengths and complement them with robust practices to build secure systems.

Leveraging Rust's Safety Guarantees

Rust's ownership system and lack of a garbage collector help eliminate entire classes of vulnerabilities:

- **Use-after-free**

- **Null pointer dereferencing**

- **Buffer overflows**

- **Data races**

By default, Rust's safe subset does not allow these errors to occur. That said, unsafe Rust and FFI interactions can still introduce vulnerabilities. Use `unsafe` sparingly and review thoroughly.

```
fn safe_access(slice: &[u8], index: usize) -> Option<u8> {

    slice.get(index).copied()

}
```

Instead of relying on unchecked indexing (which can panic), this pattern ensures safe memory access.

Avoiding Unsafe Code

The unsafe keyword is sometimes necessary for performance or FFI. However, it should be avoided unless absolutely necessary and reviewed with scrutiny. If you do need to use it:

- Document why it's safe.

- Limit unsafe blocks in scope and responsibility.

- Encapsulate unsafe logic behind safe abstractions.

Example of safe encapsulation:

```
fn get_unchecked_safe<T>(vec: &[T], index: usize) -> Option<&T> {

    if index < vec.len() {

        // SAFETY: We've manually checked bounds.

        Some(unsafe { vec.get_unchecked(index) })

    } else {

        None

    }

}
```

Here, the bounds check ensures that unsafe usage doesn't lead to memory issues.

Dependency Auditing and Supply Chain Security

Rust's ecosystem is thriving, with thousands of crates on crates.io. While using libraries is encouraged for productivity, blindly trusting dependencies is a common security risk.

Use `cargo-audit`

Install and run `cargo-audit` to detect vulnerabilities in your dependencies:

```
cargo install cargo-audit

cargo audit
```

This checks your `Cargo.lock` against the RustSec advisory database and alerts you to known CVEs and insecure versions.

Keep Dependencies Updated

Use tools like `cargo-outdated`:

```
cargo install cargo-outdated

cargo outdated
```

Update regularly and subscribe to security advisories of key libraries. Always review changelogs before upgrading major versions.

Prefer Well-Maintained Crates

When choosing third-party crates:

- Check GitHub activity (commits, issues, stars).
- Look for recent releases.
- Avoid crates with low usage or single contributors, unless necessary.
- Use `cargo crev` to crowdsource trust in dependencies.

Input Validation and Sanitization

Even with strong memory safety, your application logic must still validate and sanitize all user input to prevent:

- Injection attacks

- Logic bugs

- Resource exhaustion

Always validate untrusted data at the boundaries of your application.

```
fn validate_username(name: &str) -> Result<(), &'static str> {

    if name.len() > 32 {

        Err("Username too long")

    } else if !name.chars().all(|c| c.is_ascii_alphanumeric()) {

        Err("Username must be alphanumeric")

    } else {

        Ok(())

    }

}
```

Sanitize output for web or CLI contexts to avoid cross-site scripting or terminal injection issues.

Secure Serialization and Deserialization

Deserialization bugs can lead to critical security issues. When using serde or similar tools:

- Never deserialize untrusted data into structs with #[serde(default)] unless required.

- Prefer explicit field mapping and validation.

- Avoid untagged enums when consuming third-party inputs.

Use `serde_json::from_slice` over `from_str` for stricter parsing and better performance.

```rust
#[derive(Deserialize)]

struct LoginPayload {

    username: String,

    password: String,

}



fn process_login(data: &[u8]) -> Result<LoginPayload,
serde_json::Error> {

    serde_json::from_slice(data)

}
```

Secure Configuration Management

Never hardcode secrets (API keys, tokens, credentials) in source code or configuration files that may be version controlled. Instead:

- Use environment variables securely via crates like `dotenvy` or `config`.

- Store secrets using a secure vault (e.g., HashiCorp Vault, AWS Secrets Manager).

- Ensure secrets are never logged or printed.

```rust
use std::env;



fn load_api_key() -> Result<String, &'static str> {

    env::var("API_KEY").map_err(|_| "Missing API_KEY")
```

```
}
```

Audit your `.env`, `Cargo.toml`, and logs to ensure secrets don't leak.

Logging Without Leaking

Logging is essential for debugging and observability, but it can easily become a security liability if:

- Sensitive data is logged.

- Logs are improperly stored or exposed.

- Log levels are misconfigured in production.

Recommendations:

- Use structured logging (e.g., `tracing` or `log` crate).

- Scrub or redact personally identifiable information (PII).

- Configure different log levels for dev vs. production.

- Avoid panicking logs or stack traces that may expose internals.

Example using `tracing`:

```
use tracing::{info, warn};


info!(user_id = %user.id, "User logged in successfully.");

warn!("Failed login attempt for unknown username");
```

Authentication and Authorization

While Rust doesn't ship with a web framework, many community libraries provide authentication and authorization utilities (e.g., `jsonwebtoken`, `argon2`, `actix-web`, `axum`).

- Use proven cryptographic libraries.

- Never roll your own authentication or password hashing.

- Use argon2 or bcrypt for password storage.

- Validate JWTs strictly: check expiry, issuer, and audience.

```rust
use argon2::{self, Config};


fn hash_password(password: &str) -> String {

    let salt = b"static_salt"; // Use dynamic salt in production!

    argon2::hash_encoded(password.as_bytes(), salt,
&Config::default()).unwrap()

}
```

Integrate role-based access control or capability-based access depending on system needs.

Avoiding Denial-of-Service (DoS)

Rust's performance makes it easy to build fast services, but without safeguards, they can be vulnerable to resource exhaustion attacks:

- **Input length checks:** Avoid unbounded input parsing.

- **Concurrency limits:** Use connection pools or Semaphore.

- **Rate limiting:** Introduce per-IP rate limiting for APIs.

- **Time and memory limits:** Use watchdogs in long-running tasks.

Example of limiting file upload size:

```rust
fn validate_upload_size(bytes: &[u8]) -> Result<(), &'static str> {
```

```
if bytes.len() > 10 * 1024 * 1024 {

    Err("File too large")

} else {

    Ok(())

}

}
```

Also consider configuring OS-level ulimits and container resource limits.

Secure Build and Deployment

Secure deployment starts with a clean and reproducible build. With Rust:

- Use `cargo install --locked` or `cargo build --locked` to ensure reproducible builds.

- Compile in release mode for production (`cargo build --release`).

- Use static linking when deploying to minimal environments.

- Verify binary signatures in CI/CD pipelines.

Consider tools like:

- `sccache` for caching builds

- `docker-slim` or `distroless` for minimal images

Use TLS (HTTPS) everywhere. The `rustls` crate offers a memory-safe TLS alternative to OpenSSL.

Threat Modeling and Code Review

Perform regular threat modeling sessions with your team. Focus on:

- Entry points

- Data flows

- External integrations

- Sensitive operations

Ask questions like:

- What happens if an attacker controls this input?

- Can someone access this data without permission?

- Are we exposing internal logic or structure?

Use tools like `cargo-geiger` to scan for `unsafe` usage:

```
cargo install cargo-geiger

cargo geiger
```

Combine with code review checklists focusing on logic flaws and access control.

Keeping Up with Evolving Threats

Rust's security ecosystem is improving quickly. Stay current:

- Follow RustSec advisories (https://rustsec.org/)

- Subscribe to newsletters (e.g., "This Week in Rust")

- Participate in forums like users.rust-lang.org and security channels

Summary

Rust provides an exceptional starting point for secure software development, but security is not automatic. You must combine safe language features with thorough dependency management, input validation, access control, logging hygiene, and infrastructure hardening. By adopting a security-first mindset and layering your protections across the stack, you can build robust systems that resist both accidental bugs and deliberate attacks.

Continuous Integration and Deployment (CI/CD)

Modern software engineering teams rely on Continuous Integration and Continuous Deployment (CI/CD) to streamline delivery, reduce errors, and ship code confidently. In Rust, the strong guarantees provided by the compiler, along with robust tooling from the ecosystem, make CI/CD pipelines extremely effective and reliable. This section walks through designing, implementing, and optimizing CI/CD pipelines tailored to Rust applications — from local development to production deployment.

Principles of CI/CD

At its core, CI/CD automates the process of building, testing, and deploying code. It helps catch issues early, reduce integration pain, and enable rapid delivery cycles. The key components include:

- **Continuous Integration (CI):** Every code change is integrated, built, and tested automatically.

- **Continuous Deployment (CD):** Successfully validated code is automatically released to production.

- **Continuous Delivery:** Similar to CD, but deployment to production is a manual decision after automated checks.

With Rust, CI/CD pipelines can take full advantage of the language's determinism, safety, and static analysis tools.

Designing Your Rust CI Pipeline

Start by identifying the stages in your pipeline. A typical Rust CI pipeline includes:

1. **Code Checkout**

2. **Dependency Installation**

3. **Formatting Checks**

4. **Linting with Clippy**

5. **Running Tests**

6. **Build Artifacts**

7. **Security Audits**

8. **Optional Benchmarking**

9. **Deployment**

Each of these stages can run in isolation or be chained in a CI system like GitHub Actions, GitLab CI, CircleCI, or Jenkins.

Example: GitHub Actions Pipeline

GitHub Actions is a popular CI/CD platform with deep Rust support. Here's a complete `ci.yml` example:

```yaml
name: CI Pipeline

on:
  push:
    branches: [main]
  pull_request:
    branches: [main]

jobs:
  build:
    runs-on: ubuntu-latest

    steps:
    - uses: actions/checkout@v3

    - name: Set up Rust
      uses: actions-rs/toolchain@v1
      with:
        toolchain: stable
```

```
      override: true


  - name: Install Dependencies

    run: cargo fetch


  - name: Format Check

    run: cargo fmt --all -- --check


  - name: Lint

    run: cargo clippy --all-targets --all-features -- -D warnings


  - name: Run Tests

    run: cargo test --all --locked


  - name: Audit Dependencies

    run: |

      cargo install cargo-audit || true

      cargo audit


  - name: Build Release Binary

    run: cargo build --release
```

This config ensures:

- No formatting issues

- No linter warnings

- All tests pass

- All dependencies are secure

- A release binary is built and ready

You can add cache support to improve performance:

```
- name: Cache cargo registry

  uses: actions/cache@v3

  with:

    path: |

      ~/.cargo/registry

      ~/.cargo/git

      target

    key: ${{ runner.os }}-cargo-${{ hashFiles('**/Cargo.lock') }}
```

Formatting and Linting in CI

Rust's tooling encourages clean code through formatting (`rustfmt`) and linting (`clippy`). Automate these checks early:

```
cargo fmt --all -- --check

cargo clippy --all-targets -- -D warnings
```

Fail the build on violations. Use pre-commit hooks locally to catch them before pushing.

Running Tests

Tests form the backbone of CI. Run:

- Unit tests

- Integration tests (`tests/` directory)

- Documentation tests

Use the `--locked` flag to enforce reproducibility:

```
cargo test --all --locked
```

For test coverage, integrate `tarpaulin` (Linux only):

```
cargo install cargo-tarpaulin
cargo tarpaulin --out Html
```

Export the report for inspection or badge generation.

Security Audits in CI

Automate vulnerability scanning with `cargo-audit`:

```
cargo install cargo-audit
cargo audit
```

Fail the pipeline if known vulnerabilities exist. Optionally allow overrides with `RUSTSEC-IGNORE`.

Combine with `cargo-deny` to enforce license and advisory policies:

```
cargo install cargo-deny
```

```
cargo deny check
```

Configuration in `deny.toml` allows you to specify whitelisted licenses, allowed advisories, and banned crates.

Building Artifacts and Releases

Build your application in release mode to produce optimized binaries:

```
cargo build --release
```

Store build artifacts using your CI provider's native support. For example:

```
- name: Upload Release Artifact

  uses: actions/upload-artifact@v3

  with:

    name: my-binary

    path: target/release/my-app
```

Tag releases with Git and automatically create GitHub releases:

```
- name: Create GitHub Release

  uses: softprops/action-gh-release@v1

  with:

    files: target/release/my-app
```

Deploying Rust Applications

How you deploy depends on the target platform:

- **CLI tools:** Upload binaries to GitHub releases or distribute via package managers.

- **Web services:** Build Docker images and deploy to a container orchestrator.

- **Embedded apps:** Flash onto target hardware or ship firmware.

Example: Docker Build and Push

```
FROM rust:1.75 AS builder

WORKDIR /usr/src/app

COPY . .

RUN cargo build --release


FROM debian:buster-slim

COPY --from=builder /usr/src/app/target/release/my-app
/usr/local/bin/my-app

ENTRYPOINT ["my-app"]
```

In GitHub Actions:

```
  - name: Login to DockerHub

    uses: docker/login-action@v2

    with:

      username: ${{ secrets.DOCKER_USERNAME }}

      password: ${{ secrets.DOCKER_PASSWORD }}


  - name: Build and Push Docker Image
```

```
uses: docker/build-push-action@v4

with:

  context: .

  push: true

  tags: myorg/my-app:latest
```

Deploying to Production

For web or backend services, you may deploy to:

- **Kubernetes:** Using Helm or manifests

- **AWS ECS/Fargate:** Managed containers

- **Azure App Service:** For HTTP apps

- **DigitalOcean App Platform / Fly.io / Railway:** Developer-friendly platforms

Deployments should be:

- **Idempotent**

- **Rollback-capable**

- **Versioned**

- **Secured with auth and TLS**

Use Git tags or semantic versioning to track releases. Integrate notifications via Slack, email, or dashboards.

Monitoring and Observability

Deployment is just the beginning. Ensure observability through:

- **Structured logging:** Use `tracing` or `log`

- **Metrics collection:** With `prometheus` crate

- **Error tracking:** Integrate with Sentry or similar

- **Health checks:** HTTP endpoints or probes

Example metrics integration:

```
use prometheus::{Encoder, TextEncoder, register_counter, Counter};

lazy_static! {
    static ref REQUESTS_TOTAL: Counter =
register_counter!("requests_total", "Total requests").unwrap();
}

fn handle_request() {
    REQUESTS_TOTAL.inc();
}
```

Expose `/metrics` endpoint for Prometheus to scrape.

CI/CD for Rust Libraries

If you're publishing crates instead of apps:

- Run `cargo publish --dry-run` in CI.

- Use `cargo-release` for automated versioning and changelog generation.

- Authenticate with crates.io using API tokens.

```
- name: Publish to crates.io
    run: cargo publish --token ${{ secrets.CARGO_REGISTRY_TOKEN }}
```

Ensure `Cargo.toml` includes proper metadata, versioning, documentation, and categories.

Best Practices for CI/CD in Rust

- Use `--locked` to enforce `Cargo.lock` consistency.

- Cache `target/`, `registry/`, and `git/` folders.

- Pin tool versions (`rustup`, `cargo-audit`, etc.).

- Test with both `debug` and `release` profiles if applicable.

- Use matrix builds to test multiple Rust versions (stable, beta, nightly).

Example matrix in GitHub Actions:

```
strategy:
  matrix:
    rust: [stable, beta, nightly]
```

This ensures future-proofing and proactive break detection.

Summary

CI/CD transforms Rust's strengths into a powerful delivery mechanism. By automating formatting, testing, security checks, builds, and deployment, teams can focus on building features while maintaining high confidence in stability and security. With strong community tooling and deterministic builds, Rust offers a production-ready pipeline experience that scales with your codebase and team. Whether shipping CLI tools or web services, CI/CD is the backbone of sustainable Rust development in production.

Case Studies: Rust in Real-World Applications

Rust's journey from a systems programming curiosity to a production-grade language powering real-world applications has been extraordinary. Its memory safety, fearless concurrency, and zero-cost abstractions have made it the language of choice for mission-critical applications across various industries. In this section, we'll explore several detailed case studies of how companies and communities have adopted Rust in production, what challenges they encountered, and what benefits they reaped. These examples will demonstrate the practical power of Rust and offer insights for organizations considering similar paths.

Case Study 1: Firefox — Servo and Quantum

Organization: Mozilla
Domain: Browser Engine
Use Case: High-performance parallel rendering engine

Mozilla created Rust in part to solve the growing complexity and instability of browser engines. The Servo project was an experimental parallel browser engine written entirely in Rust, designed to push the boundaries of safety and performance.

Challenges Faced

- The need to safely run rendering code across multiple threads.

- Legacy C++ codebases were brittle and error-prone under concurrency.

- Security vulnerabilities from memory safety issues in large C++ codebases.

Rust's Role

Rust's ownership and concurrency model enabled Mozilla engineers to parallelize layout and rendering tasks without race conditions or memory leaks.

```
fn parallel_layout(dom_nodes: &[DomNode]) {

    dom_nodes.par_iter().for_each(|node| {

        layout_node(node);

    });

}
```

Using rayon, layout computation was performed in parallel. This approach significantly improved page load times without compromising safety.

Outcome

Rust's success in Servo led to its integration into Firefox's rendering engine as part of **Project Quantum**. Components such as Quantum CSS (Stylo) replaced C++ code with safe, parallel Rust. Mozilla reported measurable performance gains and reduced crashes due to memory bugs.

Case Study 2: Cloudflare — Infrastructure Services

Organization: Cloudflare
Domain: Internet Security and CDN
Use Case: Writing performant and safe edge services

Cloudflare adopted Rust to replace critical parts of its infrastructure, including DNS services and the performance-focused **Quiche** project (a QUIC protocol implementation).

Challenges Faced

- The need for low-latency, high-performance services handling massive scale.

- Avoiding the undefined behavior and unsafety of C while maintaining speed.

- Ensuring correctness under high concurrency.

Rust's Role

Cloudflare used Rust to write performance-sensitive networking code that's safe and highly concurrent. The Quiche project implemented QUIC using async/await, tokio, and mio.

```
async fn handle_connection(stream: TcpStream) -> Result<(), Error> {

    let mut quic_conn = quiche::Connection::accept(stream, ...)?;

    while let Some(packet) = quic_conn.recv().await {

        process_packet(packet).await?;

    }

    Ok(())

}
```

With zero-cost abstractions and strict memory safety, Rust allowed them to deploy reliable, fast networking code without garbage collection.

Outcome

Cloudflare engineers report that Rust has significantly improved code maintainability, testability, and reliability. In the DNS system alone, replacing C with Rust reduced crashes and improved test coverage, all while maintaining top-tier performance.

Case Study 3: Dropbox — File Synchronization Engine

Organization: Dropbox
Domain: Cloud Storage
Use Case: Rewriting the file sync engine for clients

Dropbox faced performance and complexity issues with their original file synchronization engine written in Python and Go. They needed a fast, predictable, cross-platform solution.

Challenges Faced

- Platform-specific bugs due to inconsistent behavior across OSes.

- Performance bottlenecks in Go and Python implementations.

- Complexity in testing and debugging cross-platform filesystem behavior.

Rust's Role

Rust was chosen to rewrite the sync engine for its:

- Cross-platform capabilities

- Low-level system access

- Memory safety guarantees

- Excellent tooling and testing support

```rust
fn scan_directory(path: &Path) -> io::Result<Vec<FileInfo>> {

    let mut entries = Vec::new();

    for entry in fs::read_dir(path)? {

        let entry = entry?;

        let metadata = entry.metadata()?;

        entries.push(FileInfo::from_metadata(&entry.path(),
metadata));
```

```
    }

    Ok(entries)

}
```

The new engine interfaces directly with system APIs, using Rust's strong type system to abstract OS-specific logic cleanly.

Outcome

The Rust-based engine achieved massive improvements in CPU and memory usage. Developers found it easier to test and debug, leading to faster iteration and more confident deployment cycles.

Case Study 4: Figma — Real-Time Collaborative Design

Organization: Figma
Domain: Design Software
Use Case: Replacing performance-critical pieces of backend infrastructure

Figma handles collaborative design sessions with real-time interactions among thousands of users. Their real-time data pipeline was originally written in TypeScript and suffered under high load.

Challenges Faced

- Node.js struggled with high CPU usage and garbage collection pauses.

- Serialization and deserialization were bottlenecks.

- Reducing memory usage without sacrificing performance.

Rust's Role

Figma engineers rewrote the core multiplayer server component in Rust. Rust provided deterministic performance, strong typing, and predictable memory behavior. They also used Rust's FFI to build efficient bindings to existing TypeScript interfaces.

Outcome

The Rust component processed 6x more operations per second compared to its JavaScript predecessor and used significantly less memory. Latency during peak collaboration was greatly reduced. Figma's team has continued investing in Rust, exploring further integration.

Case Study 5: Amazon Web Services — Firecracker

Organization: AWS
Domain: Cloud Computing / Virtualization
Use Case: Building microVMs for serverless platforms like Lambda

Firecracker is a virtualization tool designed by AWS to launch lightweight VMs in milliseconds. Security and performance were top priorities.

Challenges Faced

- Existing hypervisors were bloated and difficult to secure.

- Needed microsecond-scale boot times.

- Desired maximum isolation with minimal overhead.

Rust's Role

AWS chose Rust to build Firecracker for its:

- Safe systems programming

- Control over memory layout

- Absence of runtime/GC

- Strong ecosystem and compile-time correctness

```
#[repr(C)]

struct VcpuState {

    regs: [u64; 32],

    pc: u64,

    status: u64,

}
```

Low-level data structures were memory-aligned and optimized for bare-metal use. Rust allowed them to build with confidence while maintaining high speed.

Outcome

Firecracker is now used to power millions of Lambda and Fargate containers per day. Rust enabled rapid development with strong guarantees and minimal security vulnerabilities.

Common Themes and Takeaways

Across all these cases, several themes emerge:

- **Safety without Performance Penalty:** Rust consistently delivers C-level performance without sacrificing memory safety.

- **Maintainability and Readability:** Engineers report that Rust code is easier to test and debug, especially compared to C/C++.

- **Concurrency without Fear:** Multithreaded workloads are significantly easier to reason about in Rust.

- **Tooling Matters:** Tools like `clippy`, `cargo test`, and `rustfmt` contribute to developer productivity and code quality.

Lessons Learned for Adopting Rust

Based on these case studies, here are key insights for teams planning to adopt Rust:

1. **Start with a Pilot:** Identify a self-contained, performance-critical component to rewrite in Rust.

2. **Invest in Training:** Initial learning curves can be steep. Internal workshops, pair programming, and open-source contributions can help ramp up teams.

3. **Avoid Premature Abstraction:** Rust's type system can be tempting for complex abstractions. Keep things simple until necessary.

4. **Use the Ecosystem:** Rust's community crates are robust. From async runtimes to cryptography, leverage existing work.

5. **Automate Everything:** Formatting, linting, testing, and security scanning should be part of your CI from day one.

6. **Secure FFI Carefully:** When interfacing with other languages, encapsulate unsafe code, audit frequently, and document behavior.

Final Thoughts

Rust is no longer a niche or experimental language. It is a battle-tested, production-grade system capable of powering some of the world's most critical infrastructure. These real-world applications prove that Rust's core promise—**safe, fast, and productive systems**

programming—is not just theoretical. Organizations large and small are reaping tangible benefits in performance, reliability, and maintainability.

For teams seeking to future-proof their architecture or solve long-standing performance or safety issues, Rust offers a compelling path forward backed by an enthusiastic and growing community. The case studies in this section serve not only as validation of Rust's maturity but as a blueprint for how to integrate it successfully into your own production systems.

Chapter 11: Appendices

Glossary of Terms

In this section, we present an extensive glossary of terms commonly encountered in Rust programming and systems development. Whether you're a beginner looking to familiarize yourself with new concepts or an experienced developer brushing up on terminology, this glossary provides the foundational understanding necessary to navigate Rust's ecosystem effectively. The definitions provided aim to be comprehensive yet concise, with practical relevance to Rust's language features and systems programming paradigms.

Abstract Syntax Tree (AST)
A tree representation of the abstract syntactic structure of source code. In Rust, the compiler builds an AST during parsing, which is then used in subsequent stages like type checking and optimization.

Alias
An alternative name for an existing type. In Rust, you can create type aliases using the `type` keyword.

```
type Kilometers = i32;

let distance: Kilometers = 5;
```

Asynchronous Programming
A form of concurrency that enables a program to handle many tasks at once, particularly I/O-bound tasks. Rust uses `async` and `await` keywords for asynchronous code execution.

Atomicity
A property ensuring operations are performed as indivisible units. Rust provides atomic types like `AtomicUsize` in the `std::sync::atomic` module for lock-free concurrent programming.

Borrow Checker
Rust's static analysis tool that enforces ownership and borrowing rules at compile time to ensure memory safety without a garbage collector.

Box<T>
A smart pointer for heap allocation. `Box` allows for recursive data types and is commonly used when the size of a type cannot be known at compile time.

```
let b = Box::new(5);

println!("b = {}", b);
```

Cargo
Rust's package manager and build system. It simplifies building, testing, and managing dependencies.

Closure
An anonymous function that can capture variables from its enclosing scope. In Rust, closures can be assigned to variables or passed to functions.

```
let add = |a, b| a + b;

println!("{}", add(2, 3)); // Outputs: 5
```

Concurrency
Running multiple tasks seemingly at the same time. Rust supports both thread-based and async concurrency with strong guarantees around memory safety.

Crate
A compilation unit in Rust. A crate can be a binary or a library, and it corresponds to a single `Cargo.toml` file.

Data Race
A condition where two or more threads access the same memory location concurrently, and at least one of the accesses is a write. Rust prevents data races at compile time.

Dereference Operator (*)
Used to access the value a pointer is pointing to. It's often used with smart pointers like `Box`, `Rc`, and raw pointers.

```
let x = 5;

let y = &x;

assert_eq!(5, *y);
```

Drop Trait
Used to run code when a value goes out of scope. This is the foundation of Rust's deterministic resource management.

```rust
struct Droppable;

impl Drop for Droppable {

    fn drop(&mut self) {

        println!("Dropping!");

    }

}
```

Enum
A type that can be one of several variants. Enums are commonly used in pattern matching and represent a value that could be one of many types.

```rust
enum Direction {

    Up,

    Down,

    Left,

    Right,

}
```

FFI (Foreign Function Interface)
A mechanism for Rust code to interact with functions written in other languages, such as C. This is essential for systems-level integration.

```rust
extern "C" {

    fn abs(input: i32) -> i32;
```

```
}
```

Generics
Allow for type abstraction, enabling code reuse across different types. Rust generics are zero-cost and monomorphized at compile time.

```
fn identity<T>(x: T) -> T {

    x

}
```

Heap
A memory region for dynamically allocated data. Rust requires explicit heap allocation through types like Box, Vec, or String.

Immutable Reference (&T)
Allows read-only access to data. Multiple immutable references can coexist.

Lifetimes
Annotations that describe the scope for which a reference is valid. They are crucial for managing how long data should be accessible without risking use-after-free errors.

```
fn longest<'a>(x: &'a str, y: &'a str) -> &'a str {

    if x.len() > y.len() { x } else { y }

}
```

Match Expression
Rust's powerful control flow operator that allows exhaustive pattern matching.

```
let number = 7;

match number {

    1 => println!("One"),
```

```
    2 | 3 => println!("Two or Three"),

    _ => println!("Something else"),

}
```

Mutex
Mutual exclusion primitive useful for protecting shared state across threads. Rust provides `Mutex<T>` in the standard library.

Ownership
The central concept in Rust's memory model. Every value in Rust has a single owner responsible for its memory.

Pattern Matching
A mechanism that lets you compare a value against a series of patterns and deconstruct complex data types.

Pointer
A variable that holds a memory address. Rust has various pointer types including references (`&T`, `&mut T`), smart pointers (`Box`, `Rc`, `Arc`), and raw pointers.

Rc<T> (Reference Counted)
A smart pointer that enables multiple ownership of data. Not thread-safe—used for single-threaded reference counting.

RefCell<T>
A type that provides interior mutability. Used when you need mutability in an immutable context, checked at runtime.

Result<T, E>
An enum for error handling. `Ok(T)` represents success, and `Err(E)` represents failure.

```
fn divide(x: f64, y: f64) -> Result<f64, String> {

    if y == 0.0 {

        Err("Cannot divide by zero".into())

    } else {

        Ok(x / y)

    }

}
```

```
}
```

Shadowing
Re-declaring a variable with the same name, which overrides the previous binding.

```
let x = 5;

let x = x + 1;
```

Stack
A region of memory used for function call frames and local variables. Memory is allocated and deallocated in a LIFO (Last In, First Out) manner.

Struct
A custom data type that lets you group together related values.

```
struct Point {

    x: i32,

    y: i32,

}
```

Thread
A lightweight process. Rust's standard library provides facilities for spawning and managing threads with `std::thread`.

Trait
Defines shared behavior in Rust. Traits are similar to interfaces in other languages and are fundamental for polymorphism.

```
trait Speak {

    fn speak(&self);

}
```

Type Inference
Rust can often infer types, making code more concise without sacrificing type safety.

Unsafe Code
A way to perform operations that the Rust compiler can't guarantee to be safe. Requires the `unsafe` keyword and is typically used for low-level systems work.

Vector (`Vec<T>`)
A growable array type. The most commonly used collection in Rust.

```rust
let mut v = Vec::new();

v.push(1);

v.push(2);
```

WebAssembly (WASM)
A binary instruction format for a stack-based virtual machine, supported by Rust for targeting the browser and beyond.

Zero-Cost Abstraction
A principle that abstractions in Rust should have no runtime overhead compared to handwritten low-level code. The compiler eliminates unnecessary overhead during compilation.

This glossary is not just a reference but also a guide to help solidify the foundational concepts of Rust. As you progress through real-world systems projects or advanced Rust chapters, keep this section in mind to refresh key terms and deepen your understanding.

Resources for Further Learning

Mastering Rust and systems programming is a journey that goes well beyond a single book. The Rust ecosystem is rich and ever-evolving, with new tools, libraries, idioms, and patterns emerging regularly. In this section, you'll find an extensive compilation of high-quality resources—ranging from official documentation and books to video tutorials, blogs, forums, open-source projects, and curated learning paths.

Whether you are just beginning or looking to deepen your knowledge in specialized areas like async Rust, embedded systems, or WebAssembly, this section provides you with the means to continue your learning effectively.

Official Documentation

The Rust Programming Language (a.k.a. "The Book")
Link: https://doc.rust-lang.org/book/
This is the most authoritative and beginner-friendly introduction to Rust. It covers all core concepts in-depth, with examples and exercises that reinforce the learning experience.

Rust by Example
Link: https://doc.rust-lang.org/rust-by-example/
A hands-on collection of examples that demonstrate Rust syntax and idioms. It complements "The Book" by focusing more on code than explanations.

The Rust Reference
Link: https://doc.rust-lang.org/reference/
An in-depth technical reference for Rust, covering precise details of the language semantics. Ideal for advanced learners or those contributing to the compiler.

Rust Standard Library Documentation
Link: https://doc.rust-lang.org/std/
Essential for understanding how to use the powerful tools provided by Rust's standard library.

Rustonomicon
Link: https://doc.rust-lang.org/nomicon/
A guide for writing unsafe and low-level Rust code. Highly recommended for those diving into FFI, custom allocators, or OS development.

The Embedded Rust Book
Link: https://docs.rust-embedded.org/book/
Focused on using Rust for embedded development. Covers microcontrollers, no_std development, and real-time applications.

Recommended Books

Programming Rust (Jim Blandy and Jason Orendorff)
Published by O'Reilly, this book dives deeper into Rust with strong emphasis on systems programming. It explains how to use Rust's powerful features effectively in large applications.

Rust for Rustaceans (Jon Gjengset)
Geared towards intermediate and advanced Rust developers, this book explores idiomatic Rust and best practices in real-world development. Excellent for polishing your understanding of ownership, lifetimes, async, and more.

Hands-On Concurrency with Rust (Brian L. Troutwine)
Focused on building robust concurrent applications. Great companion if you're working on performance-critical or multithreaded systems.

Rust in Action (Tim McNamara)
Bridges the gap between theoretical knowledge and real-world systems projects. Explores how Rust works with low-level resources like memory, filesystems, and system calls.

Online Courses and Video Tutorials

Rust Crash Course – FreeCodeCamp
YouTube: Search "Rust Crash Course FreeCodeCamp"
A compact but comprehensive introduction to Rust aimed at developers with experience in other languages.

"Let's Get Rusty" YouTube Channel
YouTube: https://www.youtube.com/@letsgetrusty
Covers a wide variety of Rust topics, from beginner tutorials to deep dives into async, performance tuning, and popular libraries.

Second Edition of The Book – Audio/Visual Format
Available as audiobooks and videos via community contributions. Look for narrated versions on YouTube and GitHub repositories that accompany "The Book."

Udemy and Coursera Courses
While not all are free, many paid courses offer structured learning paths and come with certification. Look for high-rated instructors with practical exercises.

Blogs and Technical Articles

The New Stack
Provides stories and updates on Rust's adoption in industry, especially for backend and cloud-native systems.

Without Boats (Aaron Turon's Blog)
https://boats.gitlab.io/blog/
A deep thinker in the Rust community. Articles explore the internals of Rust, async, and trait systems.

Ferrous Systems Blog
https://ferrous-systems.com/blog/
Ferrous Systems is a consulting company that works with Rust in safety-critical systems and embedded domains. Their blog is full of insights.

Fasterthanli.me (Amos Wenger)
https://fasterthanli.me/
An excellent resource for intermediate to advanced Rust topics. Fun, narrative-driven tutorials that break down complex topics.

Forums and Community Spaces

The Rust Users Forum
https://users.rust-lang.org/
The official forum where you can ask questions, share projects, and get help from the broader Rust community.

The Rust Programming Language Subreddit
https://www.reddit.com/r/rust/
A very active subreddit where users post news, tutorials, questions, and discussions.

Rust Discord Server
https://discord.gg/rust-lang
The primary chat-based community, categorized into topics like beginner help, embedded, async, web development, and more.

Stack Overflow
Thousands of Rust-related questions are already answered, and it's a great place to search when you're stuck on a specific error or concept.

Curated Learning Paths

Rust-Lang Learning (GitHub Awesome List)
https://github.com/ctjhoa/rust-learning
A curated list of learning materials, categorized by level and focus area. Includes books, articles, talks, and projects.

Are We Learning Yet?
https://www.arewelearningyet.com/
Tracks the ecosystem's learning resources. Useful to explore what's mature and actively maintained.

Rustlings
https://github.com/rust-lang/rustlings
A hands-on series of small exercises that teach core Rust concepts interactively. Best used alongside "The Book".

Exercism.io
https://exercism.io/tracks/rust

An interactive platform with mentored exercises to learn Rust. Focuses on code quality and test-driven learning.

Open Source Projects to Learn From

Servo
A browser engine written in Rust. Originally a Mozilla project, it's a great place to study high-performance Rust in a real-world context.

Ripgrep (rg)
A blazing-fast search tool built in Rust. The codebase is clean and highly performant—ideal for learning about systems-level I/O and threading.

Alacritty
A GPU-accelerated terminal emulator. Teaches how to use low-level graphics APIs and concurrency in Rust.

Bevy
A data-driven game engine built in Rust. If you're interested in game development, Bevy's ECS (Entity-Component-System) architecture is enlightening.

Tokio
A runtime for writing reliable asynchronous applications. If you want to dive deep into async/await and concurrency, studying Tokio is essential.

Rust Editions and Language Evolution

Rust evolves steadily and thoughtfully. Each new "edition" introduces syntax improvements or ergonomics enhancements while maintaining backward compatibility. Keep up to date with:

Edition Guides
https://doc.rust-lang.org/edition-guide/
Clarifies what changes each edition brings and how to migrate older code.

RFCs (Request for Comments)
https://github.com/rust-lang/rfcs
Proposals for changes to the Rust language, libraries, and tooling. Reading accepted RFCs helps you understand why Rust works the way it does.

Industry Case Studies and Whitepapers

Dropbox: Rust in File Synchronization
Describes how Rust replaced Python and C++ components in latency-sensitive systems.

AWS Firecracker
The microVM system behind AWS Lambda and Fargate is written in Rust. Excellent example of high-performance, secure system design.

Microsoft: Rust in Windows
Microsoft has begun integrating Rust into system components for improved memory safety.

Cloudflare
Cloudflare has published several blog posts about replacing legacy C code with Rust in their edge and DNS services.

Summary

Rust's learning curve is known to be steep, but the community and resources are among the best in the software development world. With the right combination of documentation, interactive exercises, real-world projects, and community support, you can go from beginner to expert in a structured and rewarding way.

Commit to continuous learning, contribute to the community, and use these resources as your personal Rust library. Whether you're aiming to write safe embedded software, high-performance servers, or new compilers, the Rust ecosystem has the tools—and the people—to help you get there.

Sample Projects and Code Snippets

The best way to learn Rust—and systems programming in general—is to build things. This section provides a variety of sample projects and focused code snippets that demonstrate core Rust principles in action. Each project targets specific skill sets such as ownership, concurrency, networking, or embedded development. These examples are not just theoretical; they reflect practical use cases that developers commonly encounter when working with Rust.

All projects are designed to be standalone or easily extensible. Where applicable, libraries, commands, and patterns are explained in context. You are encouraged to clone, modify, and expand upon these samples as part of your learning journey.

Command-Line To-Do App

Concepts Covered: Structs, Enums, File I/O, Serialization (serde), Ownership

Dependencies:

```
[dependencies]

serde = { version = "1.0", features = ["derive"] }

serde_json = "1.0"
```

Main Components:

```rust
use serde::{Serialize, Deserialize};

use std::{fs, env, io};


#[derive(Serialize, Deserialize)]

struct Task {

    description: String,

    done: bool,

}


fn main() {

    let args: Vec<String> = env::args().collect();

    let command = args.get(1).map(String::as_str);


    let mut tasks = load_tasks();


    match command {

        Some("add") => {
```

```
            let description = args.get(2).expect("Missing task
description");

            tasks.push(Task { description: description.to_string(),
done: false });

            save_tasks(&tasks);

        },

        Some("list") => {

            for (i, task) in tasks.iter().enumerate() {

                println!("{} - [{}] {}", i, if task.done { "x" }
else { " " }, task.description);

            }

        },

        Some("done") => {

            let index: usize = args.get(2).expect("Missing task
index").parse().unwrap();

            if let Some(task) = tasks.get_mut(index) {

                task.done = true;

                save_tasks(&tasks);

            }

        },

        _ => {

            println!("Usage: todo add|list|done <arg>");

        }

    }

}
```

```rust
fn load_tasks() -> Vec<Task> {
    fs::read_to_string("tasks.json")
        .ok()
        .and_then(|data| serde_json::from_str(&data).ok())
        .unwrap_or_else(Vec::new)
}


fn save_tasks(tasks: &[Task]) {
    let data = serde_json::to_string(tasks).unwrap();
    fs::write("tasks.json", data).unwrap();
}
```

This small yet complete project demonstrates serialization, argument parsing, and basic state management in a file-based CLI application.

TCP Chat Server

Concepts Covered: Networking, Concurrency, Arc<Mutex<T>>, Threads

Dependencies: None (uses standard library only)

Highlights:

```rust
use std::io::{BufRead, BufReader, Write};
use std::net::{TcpListener, TcpStream};
use std::sync::{Arc, Mutex};
use std::thread;
```

```rust
fn handle_client(stream: TcpStream, peers:
Arc<Mutex<Vec<TcpStream>>>) {

    let mut reader = BufReader::new(&stream);

    let mut line = String::new();


    loop {

        line.clear();

        match reader.read_line(&mut line) {

            Ok(0) => break, // connection closed

            Ok(_) => {

                let message = format!("> {}", line);

                let mut peers_guard = peers.lock().unwrap();

                for peer in peers_guard.iter_mut() {

                    if peer.peer_addr().unwrap() !=
stream.peer_addr().unwrap() {

                        let _ = peer.write_all(message.as_bytes());

                    }

                }

            }

            Err(_) => break,

        }

    }


    peers.lock().unwrap().retain(|peer| peer.peer_addr().unwrap() !=
stream.peer_addr().unwrap());

}
```

```rust
fn main() {

    let listener = TcpListener::bind("127.0.0.1:9000").unwrap();

    let peers = Arc::new(Mutex::new(Vec::new()));


    for stream in listener.incoming() {

        let stream = stream.unwrap();

        let peers = Arc::clone(&peers);

        peers.lock().unwrap().push(stream.try_clone().unwrap());


        thread::spawn(move || {

            handle_client(stream, peers);

        });

    }

}
```

This project showcases Rust's approach to safe concurrency. Each client connection is handled in a separate thread, and access to the shared client list is protected using Arc<Mutex<T>>.

JSON API Server

Concepts Covered: REST APIs, Serde, Warp web framework, Async/Await

Dependencies:

```
[dependencies]

warp = "0.3"
```

```
serde = { version = "1.0", features = ["derive"] }

tokio = { version = "1", features = ["full"] }
```

Sample Implementation:

```rust
use warp::Filter;

use serde::{Deserialize, Serialize};

use std::sync::{Arc, Mutex};


#[derive(Debug, Serialize, Deserialize, Clone)]

struct User {

    id: u32,

    name: String,

}


#[tokio::main]

async fn main() {

    let users = Arc::new(Mutex::new(vec![]));


    let list_users = {

        let users = users.clone();

        warp::path("users")

            .and(warp::get())

            .map(move || warp::reply::json(&*users.lock().unwrap()))

    };
```

```rust
let add_user = {

    let users = users.clone();

    warp::path("users")

        .and(warp::post())

        .and(warp::body::json())

        .map(move |user: User| {

            users.lock().unwrap().push(user.clone());

            warp::reply::json(&user)

        })

};


let routes = list_users.or(add_user);

warp::serve(routes).run(([127, 0, 0, 1], 3030)).await;

}
```

A lightweight example of building a web service in Rust. Warp and Tokio allow writing safe, composable, asynchronous web APIs.

Embedded Blinking LED (no_std)

Concepts Covered: Embedded Rust, no_std, HAL (Hardware Abstraction Layer)

Crates Required: `cortex-m-rt`, `panic-halt`, board-specific HAL (e.g., `stm32f1xx-hal`)

```rust
#![no_std]

#![no_main]
```

```rust
use cortex_m_rt::entry;

use panic_halt as _;


use stm32f1xx_hal::{

    pac,

    prelude::*,

    delay::Delay,

};


#[entry]

fn main() -> ! {

    let dp = pac::Peripherals::take().unwrap();

    let cp = cortex_m::Peripherals::take().unwrap();


    let mut flash = dp.FLASH.constrain();

    let mut rcc = dp.RCC.constrain();


    let clocks = rcc.cfgr.freeze(&mut flash.acr);

    let mut gpio = dp.GPIOC.split();

    let mut led = gpio.pc13.into_push_pull_output(&mut gpio.crh);


    let mut delay = Delay::new(cp.SYST, clocks);
```

```
loop {

    led.set_high();

    delay.delay_ms(500_u16);

    led.set_low();

    delay.delay_ms(500_u16);

}

}
```

Though this requires hardware or emulators, it's a strong introduction to embedded systems programming. You directly manipulate GPIO, work with timing, and use no_std Rust.

WASM Calculator

Concepts Covered: WebAssembly, Front-End Integration, wasm-bindgen

Dependencies:

```
[lib]

crate-type = ["cdylib"]


[dependencies]

wasm-bindgen = "0.2"
```

Example Rust Code:

```
use wasm_bindgen::prelude::*;
```

```rust
#[wasm_bindgen]

pub fn add(a: i32, b: i32) -> i32 {

    a + b

}
```

After compiling to .wasm using wasm-pack, this function can be called from JavaScript. This is a stepping stone to more complex web-powered Rust apps.

Utility Snippets

Using Traits to Abstract Behavior:

```rust
trait Printable {

    fn print(&self);

}


impl Printable for String {

    fn print(&self) {

        println!("String: {}", self);

    }

}


impl Printable for i32 {

    fn print(&self) {

        println!("Integer: {}", self);

    }
```

```rust
}


fn display<T: Printable>(item: T) {

    item.print();

}
```

Custom Iterator Implementation:

```rust
struct Counter {

    count: u32,

}


impl Counter {

    fn new() -> Self {

        Counter { count: 0 }

    }

}


impl Iterator for Counter {

    type Item = u32;

    fn next(&mut self) -> Option<Self::Item> {

        self.count += 1;

        if self.count <= 5 {

            Some(self.count)

        } else {
```

```
        None

    }

  }

}
```

Chaining Functional Operations:

```
let numbers = vec![1, 2, 3, 4, 5];

let sum_of_squares: i32 = numbers.iter()

    .map(|x| x * x)

    .filter(|x| x % 2 == 0)

    .sum();


println!("Sum of squares: {}", sum_of_squares);
```

Summary

From CLI utilities and networked services to embedded applications and WebAssembly modules, Rust enables developers to build safe, efficient, and modern software across a wide array of domains. The examples provided here are only the beginning. You can extend each project, refactor them using crates like anyhow, thiserror, tokio, or rayon, and eventually develop full-scale applications.

Learning through building is one of the most rewarding ways to master Rust. Each line of code you write reinforces the language's principles—ownership, concurrency, performance, and safety. Use these projects as templates, inspiration, or even as the base of something larger and uniquely your own.

API Reference Guide

This section serves as a comprehensive reference for commonly used APIs in Rust's standard library and ecosystem. While Rust prides itself on a minimalist and predictable standard library, its power lies in the expressive combination of modules, traits, and data structures. The API guide below is grouped by functionality—covering core primitives, collections, concurrency, file I/O, error handling, and external crates that are foundational to professional Rust development.

Each subsection provides usage patterns, type signatures, and idiomatic code examples to demonstrate real-world applicability. This guide will help you navigate the Rust API landscape with clarity and purpose.

Core Language Primitives

Option<T>

The Option type is used when a value might be present or absent. It prevents null pointer exceptions and forces explicit handling.

```
fn find_index(vec: &[i32], value: i32) -> Option<usize> {

    for (i, &item) in vec.iter().enumerate() {

        if item == value {

            return Some(i);

        }

    }

    None

}


let idx = find_index(&[1, 2, 3], 2);

match idx {

    Some(i) => println!("Found at index {}", i),

    None => println!("Not found"),
```

```
}
```

`Result<T, E>`

Encapsulates success (Ok) or error (Err) values.

```
fn divide(a: f64, b: f64) -> Result<f64, String> {

    if b == 0.0 {

        Err("Cannot divide by zero".to_string())

    } else {

        Ok(a / b)

    }

}
```

Methods like `.map()`, `.and_then()`, and `.unwrap_or_else()` are useful for chaining and handling.

Collections

`Vec<T>`

A dynamically resizable array.

```
let mut nums = vec![1, 2, 3];

nums.push(4);

nums.remove(0);
```

Useful methods: push, pop, iter, retain, sort_by, extend, drain, into_iter

HashMap<K, V>

A hash-based key-value store.

```rust
use std::collections::HashMap;


let mut scores = HashMap::new();

scores.insert("Alice", 10);

scores.insert("Bob", 15);


if let Some(score) = scores.get("Alice") {

    println!("Score: {}", score);

}
```

Traits like Eq and Hash must be implemented for keys.

HashSet<T>

A collection of unique values.

```rust
use std::collections::HashSet;


let mut set = HashSet::new();

set.insert(1);

set.insert(2);

set.insert(2); // Won't be added again


assert_eq!(set.contains(&1), true);
```

File and IO Handling

std::fs and std::io

Rust provides rich file and I/O APIs in its standard library.

```rust
use std::fs::File;
use std::io::{Read, Write};

let mut file = File::create("hello.txt")?;
file.write_all(b"Hello, world!")?;

let mut contents = String::new();
File::open("hello.txt")?.read_to_string(&mut contents)?;
```

Other useful modules:

- BufReader, BufWriter for buffered I/O
- copy, read_dir, create_dir_all, remove_file for file system manipulation

stdin, stdout, stderr

For user interaction or terminal output.

```rust
use std::io::{self, Write};

print!("Enter name: ");
```

```rust
io::stdout().flush().unwrap();
```

```rust
let mut name = String::new();

io::stdin().read_line(&mut name).unwrap();

println!("Hello, {}", name.trim());
```

Concurrency APIs

`std::thread`

Rust's native support for spawning threads.

```rust
use std::thread;
```

```rust
let handle = thread::spawn(|| {

    println!("Running in another thread");

});

handle.join().unwrap();
```

Data sharing is safe via `Arc` and `Mutex`.

`Arc<T>` and `Mutex<T>`

Used to share mutable data across threads safely.

```rust
use std::sync::{Arc, Mutex};

use std::thread;
```

```
let counter = Arc::new(Mutex::new(0));

let mut handles = vec![];

for _ in 0..10 {
    let counter = Arc::clone(&counter);
    handles.push(thread::spawn(move || {
        let mut num = counter.lock().unwrap();
        *num += 1;
    }));
}

for handle in handles {
    handle.join().unwrap();
}

println!("Counter: {}", *counter.lock().unwrap());
```

Iterators and Closures

Iterator Trait

The heart of Rust's collection processing.

```
let nums = vec![1, 2, 3];
let squared: Vec<_> = nums.iter().map(|x| x * x).collect();
```

Chaining operations: `map`, `filter`, `fold`, `enumerate`, `zip`, `take_while`, `skip`

Closures

Anonymous functions capturing the surrounding scope.

```
let multiply = |a, b| a * b;

println!("{}", multiply(4, 5));
```

You can specify types for clarity:

```
let compare = |a: i32, b: i32| a == b;
```

Traits and Generics

Defining Traits

```
trait Greet {

    fn greet(&self) -> String;

}


struct Person;

impl Greet for Person {

    fn greet(&self) -> String {

        "Hello!".to_string()

    }
```

```
}
```

Using Generics

```
fn largest<T: PartialOrd>(list: &[T]) -> &T {

    let mut largest = &list[0];

    for item in list {

        if item > largest {

            largest = item;

        }

    }

    largest

}
```

Error Handling

? Operator

Shortcuts error propagation:

```
fn read_file() -> std::io::Result<String> {

    let mut file = std::fs::File::open("notes.txt")?;

    let mut contents = String::new();

    file.read_to_string(&mut contents)?;

    Ok(contents)

}
```

Custom Error Types

```rust
use std::fmt;

#[derive(Debug)]
struct MyError;

impl fmt::Display for MyError {
    fn fmt(&self, f: &mut fmt::Formatter) -> fmt::Result {
        write!(f, "Something went wrong")
    }
}

impl std::error::Error for MyError {}
```

Use crates like anyhow or thiserror to simplify error handling in large projects.

Macros

`println!`, `format!`, `vec!`

Built-in macros that expand into efficient code.

```rust
let greeting = format!("Hello, {}!", "Rust");
println!("{}", greeting);
```

Custom Macros

```rust
macro_rules! say_hello {
    () => {
        println!("Hello from macro!");
    };
}
```

Invoke with:

```rust
say_hello!();
```

Crates for Real-World Use

`serde`

Serialization and deserialization framework. Used with `serde_json`, `serde_yaml`, etc.

```rust
use serde::{Serialize, Deserialize};
```

```rust
#[derive(Serialize, Deserialize)]
struct User {
    name: String,
    age: u8,
}
```

tokio

Asynchronous runtime for networking, timers, tasks, and more.

```rust
#[tokio::main]
async fn main() {
    let body = reqwest::get("https://httpbin.org/get")
        .await.unwrap()
        .text().await.unwrap();
    println!("{}", body);
}
```

rayon

Data-parallelism made easy.

```rust
use rayon::prelude::*;

let nums: Vec<i32> = (1..1_000_000).collect();
let sum: i32 = nums.par_iter().sum();
```

clap

Command-line argument parsing.

```rust
use clap::Parser;


#[derive(Parser)]
```

```
struct Args {

    #[arg(short, long)]

    name: String,

}


fn main() {

    let args = Args::parse();

    println!("Hello, {}", args.name);

}
```

Working with Dates and Time

`chrono`

Date and time handling library.

```
use chrono::prelude::*;


let local: DateTime<Local> = Local::now();

println!("Local time: {}", local);
```

`std::time`

For measuring durations and delays.

```
use std::time::Instant;
```

```rust
let now = Instant::now();

// some work...

let elapsed = now.elapsed();

println!("Elapsed: {:.2?}", elapsed);
```

Summary

The Rust API ecosystem is deep, cohesive, and continuously growing. This reference guide provided a roadmap through the most critical APIs across domains—from basic collection manipulation and error handling to concurrency, asynchronous programming, file I/O, and procedural macros.

As you continue building Rust applications, you'll frequently revisit these APIs. They are the core building blocks of high-quality, performant, and safe software. Bookmark this guide, extend it with your personal notes, and use it to reinforce your mastery over Rust's expressive standard library and ecosystem.

Frequently Asked Questions

The Rust ecosystem is vast, and even experienced developers often encounter questions as they work through real-world applications. This FAQ covers both technical and conceptual challenges, with practical advice, clarifications, and best practices. These answers address the common pitfalls and nuances of the Rust language, helping you reinforce your understanding and navigate complex scenarios confidently.

What is Ownership, and Why Is It So Important?

Ownership is the foundational concept that allows Rust to manage memory without a garbage collector. Every value has a single owner (binding). When the owner goes out of scope, the value is automatically dropped.

```rust
let s1 = String::from("hello");

let s2 = s1; // s1 is moved

// println!("{}", s1); // This would cause a compile-time error
```

This system guarantees memory safety at compile time and eliminates dangling pointers and double-frees.

To maintain ownership while allowing access, use **borrowing**:

```
fn print(s: &String) {

    println!("{}", s);

}
```

Use **mut references** for writable borrowing, but only one mutable reference can exist at a time to avoid data races.

How Do Lifetimes Work?

Lifetimes ensure references are valid for as long as they are used. While Rust often infers them, explicit lifetimes help clarify the relationship between references:

```
fn longest<'a>(a: &'a str, b: &'a str) -> &'a str {

    if a.len() > b.len() { a } else { b }

}
```

In this function, both inputs and the return value share the same lifetime 'a, ensuring the returned reference doesn't outlive either input.

Lifetimes don't affect runtime behavior; they are purely compile-time constructs to ensure safety.

When Should I Use Box, Rc, or Arc?

- Box<T>: Heap allocation of a single owner. Useful for recursive types or trait objects.

```
enum List {

    Cons(i32, Box<List>),

    Nil,

}
```

- Rc<T>: Multiple ownership in a single-threaded context. It uses reference counting.

```
use std::rc::Rc;

let a = Rc::new(String::from("Shared"));
let b = Rc::clone(&a);
```

- Arc<T>: Same as Rc, but thread-safe. Often paired with Mutex<T>.

```
use std::sync::{Arc, Mutex};

let data = Arc::new(Mutex::new(5));
let d1 = Arc::clone(&data);
```

Choose based on whether the data is shared across threads (Arc) or within a single thread (Rc).

Why Can't I Borrow a Value as Mutable and Immutable at the Same Time?

This is Rust's compile-time guarantee to prevent race conditions. You either have:

- One mutable reference (`&mut T`)

- Or multiple immutable references (`&T`)

But not both at the same time.

```
let mut x = 5;

let r1 = &x;

let r2 = &x;

// let r3 = &mut x; // ERROR: cannot borrow as mutable because of
existing immutable borrows
```

This ensures memory is accessed safely and predictably without runtime overhead.

What Is the Difference Between `.clone()` and Copy Types?

- **Copy types** (`i32`, `bool`, `char`, etc.) are duplicated automatically.

- `.clone()` creates a deep copy, used when data is heap-allocated (like `String`, `Vec`, `HashMap`).

```
let a = String::from("hello");

let b = a.clone(); // Creates a new heap-allocated copy
```

Implement `Clone` manually if you need custom logic.

```
#[derive(Clone)]
```

```
struct MyData {

    name: String,

    value: i32,

}
```

How Do I Handle Errors Properly?

Rust uses `Result<T, E>` for recoverable errors and `panic!` for unrecoverable ones.

Idiomatic error handling often involves the `?` operator:

```
fn read_file() -> std::io::Result<String> {

    let mut f = std::fs::File::open("file.txt")?;

    let mut content = String::new();

    f.read_to_string(&mut content)?;

    Ok(content)

}
```

In large applications, use libraries like `thiserror`, `anyhow`, or `eyre` to handle complex error types gracefully.

What Is `unsafe` and When Should I Use It?

`unsafe` blocks allow you to bypass Rust's strict safety checks. This is necessary when:

- Calling C functions (FFI)
- Dereferencing raw pointers

- Accessing union fields

- Implementing unsafe traits

- Using inline assembly

```
unsafe {

    let ptr = &10 as *const i32;

    println!("Value: {}", *ptr);

}
```

Only use unsafe when you're certain the code cannot lead to undefined behavior. Encapsulate unsafe blocks inside safe abstractions whenever possible.

How Does Async Work in Rust?

Rust's async model is based on **futures** and **polling**. The async fn keyword returns a Future, which does nothing until awaited.

```
async fn say_hello() {

    println!("Hello async");

}
```

```
#[tokio::main]

async fn main() {

    say_hello().await;

}
```

To use async, a runtime like `tokio` or `async-std` is required. Most I/O-related crates have async versions (e.g., `reqwest`, `sqlx`, `warp`).

Key traits:

- `Future`

- `AsyncRead`, `AsyncWrite` from `tokio::io`

What Is the dyn Keyword?

Used for **trait objects**—enabling dynamic dispatch at runtime.

```
trait Shape {

    fn area(&self) -> f64;

}
```

```
fn print_area(shape: &dyn Shape) {

    println!("Area: {}", shape.area());

}
```

Use dyn when you want heterogeneous collections or runtime polymorphism. Trait objects must be object-safe (no generic methods or `Self` return types).

How Can I Create a Generic Function?

Generics allow code reuse for any type that meets the specified trait bounds.

```
fn max<T: PartialOrd>(a: T, b: T) -> T {

    if a > b { a } else { b }
```

}

Trait bounds ensure only valid operations are allowed. For complex constraints, use `where` clauses:

```
fn show<T>(item: T)

where T: std::fmt::Display {

    println!("{}", item);

}
```

What Does `'static` Mean?

The `'static` lifetime means the data lives for the **entire duration of the program**.

```
fn get_str() -> &'static str {

    "I live forever"

}
```

It's often used in thread closures or global data.

In async programming, `'static` is required because tasks can outlive their creators.

What's the Difference Between `.iter()`, `.into_iter()`, and `.iter_mut()`?

- `.iter()`: Immutable references to elements

- `.iter_mut()`: Mutable references

- `.into_iter()`: Takes ownership

```
let v = vec![1, 2, 3];

for val in v.iter() {
    println!("{}", val); // val: &i32
}


for val in v.into_iter() {
    println!("{}", val); // val: i32
}


let mut v = vec![1, 2, 3];
for val in v.iter_mut() {
    *val += 1; // val: &mut i32
}
```

How Do I Organize Large Projects?

Use mod, pub, and use to create module hierarchies:

```
mod math {
    pub fn square(x: i32) -> i32 {
        x * x
```

```
    }

}
```

```
fn main() {

    println!("{}", math::square(4));

}
```

Split files:

- `mod.rs`: Module root

- `lib.rs` / `main.rs`: Entry points

- `src/`: Each submodule in its own file or folder

Also, leverage `Cargo.toml` for defining dependencies, features, and packages.

How Can I Write Unit Tests?

Rust includes testing in its toolchain. Use the `#[test]` attribute.

```
#[cfg(test)]

mod tests {

    use super::*;


    #[test]

    fn test_addition() {

        assert_eq!(2 + 2, 4);

    }
```

```
}
```

Run with:

```
cargo test
```

Use `assert_eq!`, `assert!`, `assert_ne!`, or custom test frameworks like `rstest` or `proptest` for property testing.

Summary

This FAQ addressed foundational and advanced questions faced by Rust developers across experience levels. As Rust continues to mature, these core principles and practices remain relevant. Keep experimenting, reading the docs, and asking the right questions—the Rustacean way is to learn continuously and build fearlessly.

www.ingramcontent.com/pod-product-compliance
Lightning Source LLC
LaVergne TN
LVHW051421050326
832903LV00030BC/2927